POST-SYNODAL APOSTOLIC EXHORTATION

AMORIS LÆTITIA

OF THE HOLY FATHER

FRANCIS

TO BISHOPS, PRIESTS AND DEACONS
CONSECRATED PERSONS
CHRISTIAN MARRIED COUPLES
AND ALL THE LAY FAITHFUL

ON LOVE IN THE FAMILY

*All documents are published thanks to the generous support
of the members of the Catholic Truth Society*

CATHOLIC TRUTH SOCIETY
PUBLISHERS TO THE HOLY SEE

First published 2016 by The Incorporated Catholic Truth Society 40-46 Harleyford Road London SE11 5AY Libreria Editrice Vaticana omnia sibi vindicate iura. Sine eiusdem licentia scripto data nemini liceat hunc Amoris Lætitia denuo imprimere aut in aliam linguam vertere. Copyright © 2016 Libreria Editrice Vaticana, Citta del Vaticano. This edition Copyright © 2016 The Incorporated Catholic Truth Society.

ISBN 978 1 78469 122 6

CONTENTS

CHAPTER FOUR
LOVE IN MARRIAGE [89] 48

CHAPTER FIVE
LOVE MADE FRUITFUL [165]. 80

CHAPTER SIX
SOME PASTORAL PERSPECTIVES [199] 96

THE JOY OF LOVE

1. THE JOY OF LOVE experienced by families is also the joy of the Church. As the Synod Fathers noted, for all the many signs of crisis in the institution of marriage, "the desire to marry and form a family remains vibrant, especially among young people, and this is an inspiration to the Church".[1] As a response to that desire, "the Christian proclamation on the family is good news indeed".[2]

2. The Synod process allowed for an examination of the situation of families in today's world, and thus for a broader vision and a renewed awareness of the importance of marriage and the family. The complexity of the issues that arose revealed the need for continued open discussion of a number of doctrinal, moral, spiritual and pastoral questions. The thinking of pastors and theologians, if faithful to the Church, honest, realistic and creative, will help us to achieve greater clarity. The debates carried on in the media, in certain publications and even among the Church's ministers, range from an immoderate desire for total change without sufficient reflection or grounding, to an attitude that would solve everything by applying general rules or deriving undue conclusions from particular theological considerations.

3. Since "time is greater than space", I would make it clear that not all discussions of doctrinal, moral or pastoral issues need to be settled by interventions of the magisterium. Unity of teaching and practice is certainly necessary in the Church, but this does not preclude various ways of interpreting some aspects of that teaching or drawing certain consequences from it. This will always be the case as the Spirit guides us towards the entire truth (cf. *Jn* 16:13), until he leads us fully into the mystery of Christ and enables us to see all things as he does. Each country or region, moreover, can seek solutions better suited to its culture and

---

[1] THIRD EXTRAORDINARY GENERAL ASSEMBLY OF THE SYNOD OF BISHOPS, *Relatio Synodi* (18 October 2014), 2.

[2] FOURTEENTH ORDINARY GENERAL ASSEMBLY OF THE SYNOD OF BISHOPS, *Relatio Finalis* (24 October 2015), 3.

sensitive to its traditions and local needs. For "cultures are in fact quite diverse and every general principle... needs to be inculturated, if it is to be respected and applied".[3]

4. I must also say that the Synod process proved both impressive and illuminating. I am grateful for the many contributions that helped me to appreciate more fully the problems faced by families throughout the world. The various interventions of the Synod Fathers, to which I paid close heed, made up, as it were, a multifaceted gem reflecting many legitimate concerns and honest questions. For this reason, I thought it appropriate to prepare a post-synodal Apostolic Exhortation to gather the contributions of the two recent Synods on the family, while adding other considerations as an aid to reflection, dialogue and pastoral practice, and as a help and encouragement to families in their daily commitments and challenges.

5. This Exhortation is especially timely in this Jubilee Year of Mercy. First, because it represents an invitation to Christian families to value the gifts of marriage and the family, and to persevere in a love strengthened by the virtues of generosity, commitment, fidelity and patience. Second, because it seeks to encourage everyone to be a sign of mercy and closeness wherever family life remains imperfect or lacks peace and joy.

6. I will begin with an opening chapter inspired by the Scriptures, to set a proper tone. I will then examine the actual situation of families, in order to keep firmly grounded in reality. I will go on to recall some essential aspects of the Church's teaching on marriage and the family, thus paving the way for two central chapters dedicated to love. I will then highlight some pastoral approaches that can guide us in building sound and fruitful homes in accordance with God's plan, with a full chapter devoted to the raising

---

[3] *Concluding Address of the Fourteenth Ordinary General Assembly of the Synod of Bishops* (24 October 2015): *L'Osservatore Romano*, 26-27 October 2015, p. 13; cf. PONTIFICAL BIBLICAL COMMISSION, *Fede e cultura alla luce della Bibbia. Atti della sessione plenaria 1979 della Pontificia Commissione Biblica*, Turin, 1981; SECOND VATICAN ECUMENICAL COUNCIL, Pastoral Constitution on the Church in the Modern World *Gaudium et Spes*, 44; JOHN PAUL II, Encyclical Letter *Redemptoris Missio* (7 December 1990), 52: AAS 83 (1991), 300; Apostolic Exhortation *Evangelii Gaudium* (24 November 2013), 69, 117: AAS 105 (2013), 1049, 1068-69.

of children. Finally, I will offer an invitation to mercy and the pastoral discernment of those situations that fall short of what the Lord demands of us, and conclude with a brief discussion of family spirituality.

7. Given the rich fruits of the two-year Synod process, this Exhortation will treat, in different ways, a wide variety of questions. This explains its inevitable length. Consequently, I do not recommend a rushed reading of the text. The greatest benefit, for families themselves and for those engaged in the family apostolate, will come if each part is read patiently and carefully, or if attention is paid to the parts dealing with their specific needs. It is likely, for example, that married couples will be more concerned with Chapters Four and Five, and pastoral ministers with Chapter Six, while everyone should feel challenged by Chapter Eight. It is my hope that, in reading this text, all will feel called to love and cherish family life, for "families are not a problem; they are first and foremost an opportunity".[4]

---

[4] *Address at the Meeting of Families in Santiago de Cuba* (22 September 2015): *L'Osservatore Romano*, 24 September 2015, p. 7.

CHAPTER ONE

IN THE LIGHT OF THE WORD

8. The Bible is full of families, births, love stories and family crises. This is true from its very first page, with the appearance of Adam and Eve's family with all its burden of violence but also its enduring strength (cf. *Gen* 4) to its very last page, where we behold the wedding feast of the Bride and the Lamb (*Rev* 21:2, 9). Jesus' description of the two houses, one built on rock and the other on sand (cf. *Mt* 7:24-27), symbolizes any number of family situations shaped by the exercise of their members' freedom, for, as the poet says, "every home is a lampstand".[5] Let us now enter one of those houses, led by the Psalmist with a song that even today resounds in both Jewish and Christian wedding liturgies:

> Blessed is every one who fears the Lord,
> who walks in his ways!

> You shall eat the fruit of the labour of your hands;
> you shall be happy, and it shall go well with you.
> Your wife will be like a fruitful vine
> within your house;
> your children will be like olive shoots
> round your table.
> Thus shall the man be blessed
> who fears the Lord.
> The Lord bless you from Zion!
> May you see the prosperity of Jerusalem
> all the days of your life!
> May you see your children's children!

> Peace be upon Israel!
> (*Ps* 128:1-6).

---

[5] JORGE LUIS BORGES, "Calle Desconocida", in *Fervor de Buenos Aires*, Buenos Aires, 2011, 23.

YOU AND YOUR WIFE

9. Let us cross the threshold of this tranquil home, with its family sitting around the festive table. At the centre we see the father and mother, a couple with their personal story of love. They embody the primordial divine plan clearly spoken of by Christ himself: "Have you not read that he who made them from the beginning made them male and female?" (*Mt* 19:4). We hear an echo of the command found in the Book of Genesis: "Therefore a man shall leave his father and mother and cleave to his wife, and they shall become one flesh (*Gen* 2:24)".

10. The majestic early chapters of Genesis present the human couple in its deepest reality. Those first pages of the Bible make a number of very clear statements. The first, which Jesus paraphrases, says that "God created man in his own image, in the image of God he created them; male and female he created them" (1:27). It is striking that the "image of God" here refers to the couple, "male and female". Does this mean that sex is a property of God himself, or that God has a divine female companion, as some ancient religions held? Naturally, the answer is no. We know how clearly the Bible rejects as idolatrous such beliefs, found among the Canaanites of the Holy Land. God's transcendence is preserved, yet inasmuch as he is also the Creator, the fruitfulness of the human couple is a living and effective "image", a visible sign of his creative act.

11. The couple that loves and begets life is a true, living icon - not an idol like those of stone or gold prohibited by the Decalogue - capable of revealing God the Creator and Saviour. For this reason, fruitful love becomes a symbol of God's inner life (cf. *Gen* 1:28; 9:7; 17:2-5, 16; 28:3; 35:11; 48:3-4). This is why the Genesis account, following the "priestly tradition", is interwoven with various genealogical accounts (cf. 4:17-22, 25-26; 5; 10; 11:10-32; 25:1-4, 12-17, 19-26; 36). The ability of human couples to beget life is the path along which the history of salvation progresses. Seen this way, the couple's fruitful relationship becomes an image for understanding and describing the mystery of God himself, for in the Christian vision of the Trinity, God is contemplated as Father, Son and Spirit of love. The triune God is a communion of love, and the family is its living reflection. Saint John Paul II shed light on this when he said,

11

"Our God in his deepest mystery is not solitude, but a family, for he has within himself fatherhood, sonship and the essence of the family, which is love. That love, in the divine family, is the Holy Spirit".[6] The family is thus not unrelated to God's very being.[7] This Trinitarian dimension finds expression in the theology of Saint Paul, who relates the couple to the "mystery" of the union of Christ and the Church (cf. *Eph* 5:21-33).

12. In speaking of marriage, Jesus refers us to yet another page of Genesis, which, in its second chapter, paints a splendid and detailed portrait of the couple. First, we see the man, who anxiously seeks "a helper fit for him" (vv. 18, 20), capable of alleviating the solitude which he feels amid the animals and the world around him. The original Hebrew suggests a direct encounter, face to face, eye to eye, in a kind of silent dialogue, for where love is concerned, silence is always more eloquent than words. It is an encounter with a face, a "thou", who reflects God's own love and is man's "best possession, a helper fit for him and a pillar of support", in the words of the biblical sage (*Sir* 36:24). Or again, as the woman of the Song of Solomon will sing in a magnificent profession of love and mutual self-bestowal: "My beloved is mine and I am his… I am my beloved's and my beloved is mine" (2:16; 6:3).

13. This encounter, which relieves man's solitude, gives rise to new birth and to the family. Significantly, Adam, who is also the man of every time and place, together with his wife, starts a new family. Jesus speaks of this by quoting the passage from Genesis: "The man shall be joined to his wife, and the two shall become one" (*Mt* 19:5; cf. *Gen* 2:24). The very word "to be joined" or "to cleave", in the original Hebrew, bespeaks a profound harmony, a closeness both physical and interior, to such an extent that the word is used to describe our union with God: "My soul clings to you" (*Ps* 63:8). The marital union is thus evoked not only in its sexual and corporal dimension, but also in its voluntary self-giving in love. The result of this union is that the two "become one flesh", both physically and in the union of their hearts and lives, and, eventually, in

---

[6] *Homily at the Eucharistic Celebration in Puebla de los Ángeles* (28 January 1979), 2: AAS 71 (1979), 184.

[7] Cf. *ibid.*

a child, who will share not only genetically but also spiritually in the "flesh" of both parents.

YOUR CHILDREN ARE AS THE SHOOTS OF AN OLIVE TREE

14. Let us once more take up the song of the Psalmist. In the home where husband and wife are seated at table, children appear at their side "like olive shoots" (*Ps* 128:3), that is, full of energy and vitality. If the parents are in some sense the foundations of the home, the children are like the "living stones" of the family (cf. *1 Pet* 2:5). Significantly, the word which appears most frequently in the Old Testament after the name of God (*YHWH*, "the Lord"), is "child" (*ben,* "son"), which is itself related to the verb "to build" (*banah*). Hence, Psalm 128, in speaking of the gift of children, uses imagery drawn from the building of a house and the social life of cities: "Unless the Lord builds the house, those who build it labour in vain… Lo, sons are a heritage from the Lord, the fruit of the womb, a reward. Like arrows in the hand of a warrior are the sons of one's youth. Happy is the man who has his quiver full of them! He shall not be put to shame when he speaks with his enemies in the gate" (*Ps* 127:1, 3-5). These images reflect the culture of an ancient society, yet the presence of children is a sign of the continuity of the family throughout salvation history, from generation to generation.

15. Here too, we can see another aspect of the family. We know that the New Testament speaks of "churches that meet in homes" (cf. *1 Cor* 16:19; *Rom* 16:5; *Col* 4:15; *Philem* 2). A family's living space could turn into a domestic church, a setting for the Eucharist, the presence of Christ seated at its table. We can never forget the image found in the Book of Revelation, where the Lord says: "Behold, I stand at the door and knock; if any one hears my voice and opens the door, I will come in to him and eat with him, and he with me" (*Rev* 3:20). Here we see a home filled with the presence of God, common prayer and every blessing. This is the meaning of the conclusion of Psalm 128, which we cited above: "Thus shall the man be blessed who fears the Lord. The Lord bless you from Zion!" (*Ps* 128:4-5).

16. The Bible also presents the family as the place where children are brought up in the faith. This is evident from the description of the

13

Passover celebration (cf. *Ex* 12:26-27; *Deut* 6:20-25) and it later appears explicitly in the Jewish *haggadah*, the dialogue accompanying the rite of the Passover meal. One of the Psalms celebrates the proclamation of faith within families: "All that we have heard and known, that our fathers have told us, we will not hide from their children, but tell to the coming generation the glorious deeds of the Lord, and his might, and the wonders which he has wrought. He established a testimony in Jacob, and appointed a law in Israel, which he commanded our fathers to teach to their children; that the next generation might know them, the children yet unborn, and arise and tell them to their children" (*Ps* 78:3-6). The family is thus the place where parents become their children's first teachers in the faith. They learn this "trade", passing it down from one person to another: "When in time to come your son asks you... You shall say to him..." (*Ex* 13:14). Thus succeeding generations can raise their song to the Lord: "young men and maidens together, old and young together!"(*Ps* 148:12).

17. Parents have a serious responsibility for this work of education, as the Biblical sages often remind us (cf. *Prov* 3:11-12; 6:20-22; 13:1; 22:15; 23:13-14; 29:17). Children, for their part, are called to accept and practice the commandment: "Honour your father and your mother" (*Ex* 20:12). Here the verb "to honour" has to do with the fulfilment of family and social commitments; these are not to be disregarded under the pretence of religious motives (cf. *Mk* 7:11-13). "Whoever honours his father atones for sins, and whoever glorifies his mother is like one who lays up treasure" (*Sir* 3:3-4).

18. The Gospel goes on to remind us that children are not the property of a family, but have their own lives to lead. Jesus is a model of obedience to his earthly parents, placing himself under their charge (cf. *Lk* 2:51), but he also shows that children's life decisions and their Christian vocation may demand a parting for the sake of the Kingdom of God (cf. *Mt* 10:34-37; *Lk* 9:59-62). Jesus himself, at twelve years of age, tells Mary and Joseph that he has a greater mission to accomplish apart from his earthly family (cf. *Lk* 2:48-50). In this way, he shows the need for other, deeper bonds even within the family: "My mother and my brethren are those who

14

hear the word of God and do it" (*Lk* 8:21). All the same, in the concern he shows for children - whom the societies of the ancient Near East viewed as subjects without particular rights and even as family property - Jesus goes so far as to present them as teachers, on account of their simple trust and spontaneity towards others. "Truly I say to you, unless you turn and become like children, you will never enter the kingdom of heaven. Whoever humbles himself like this child, he is the greatest in the kingdom of heaven" (*Mt* 18:3-4).

A PATH OF SUFFERING AND BLOOD

19. The idyllic picture presented in Psalm 128 is not at odds with a bitter truth found throughout sacred Scripture, that is, the presence of pain, evil and violence that break up families and their communion of life and love. For good reason Christ's teaching on marriage (cf. *Mt* 19:3-9) is inserted within a dispute about divorce. The word of God constantly testifies to that sombre dimension already present at the beginning, when, through sin, the relationship of love and purity between man and woman turns into domination: "Your desire shall be for your husband, and he shall rule over you" (*Gen* 3:16).

20. This thread of suffering and bloodshed runs through numerous pages of the Bible, beginning with Cain's murder of his brother Abel. We read of the disputes between the sons and the wives of the Patriarchs Abraham, Isaac and Jacob, the tragedies and violence marking the family of David, the family problems reflected in the story of Tobias and the bitter complaint of Job: "He has put my brethren far from me... my kinsfolk and my close friends have failed me... I am repulsive to my wife, loathsome to the sons of my own mother" (*Job* 19:13-14, 17).

21. Jesus himself was born into a modest family that soon had to flee to a foreign land. He visits the home of Peter, whose mother-in-law is ill (cf. *Mk* 1:30-31) and shows sympathy upon hearing of deaths in the homes of Jairus and Lazarus (cf. *Mk* 5:22-24, 35-43; *Jn* 11:1-44). He hears the desperate wailing of the widow of Nain for her dead son (cf. *Lk* 7:11-15) and heeds the plea of the father of an epileptic child in a small country town (cf. *Mk* 9:17-27). He goes to the homes of tax

15

collectors like Matthew and Zacchaeus (cf. *Mt* 9:9-13; *Lk* 19:1-10), and speaks to sinners like the woman in the house of Simon the Pharisee (cf. *Lk* 7:36-50). Jesus knows the anxieties and tensions experienced by families and he weaves them into his parables: children who leave home to seek adventure (cf. *Lk* 15:11-32), or who prove troublesome (*Mt* 21:28-31) or fall prey to violence (*Mk* 12:1-9). He is also sensitive to the embarrassment caused by the lack of wine at a wedding feast (*Jn* 2:1-10), the failure of guests to come to a banquet (*Mt* 22:1-10), and the anxiety of a poor family over the loss of a coin (*Lk* 15:8-10).

22. In this brief review, we can see that the word of God is not a series of abstract ideas but rather a source of comfort and companionship for every family that experiences difficulties or suffering. For it shows them the goal of their journey, when God "will wipe away every tear from their eyes, and death shall be no more, neither shall there be mourning nor crying nor pain any more" (*Rev* 21:4).

THE WORK OF YOUR HANDS

23. At the beginning of Psalm 128, the father appears as a labourer who by the work of his hands sustains the physical well-being and tranquillity of his family: "You shall eat the fruit of the labour of your hands; you shall be happy, and it shall be well with you" (*Ps* 128:2). It is clear from the very first pages of the Bible that work is an essential part of human dignity; there we read that "the Lord God took the man and put him in the garden of Eden to till it and keep it" (*Gen* 2:15). Man is presented as a labourer who works the earth, harnesses the forces of nature and produces "the bread of anxious toil" (*Ps* 127:2), in addition to cultivating his own gifts and talents.

24. Labour also makes possible the development of society and provides for the sustenance, stability and fruitfulness of one's family: "May you see the prosperity of Jerusalem all the days of your life! May you see your children's children!" (*Ps* 128:5-6). The Book of Proverbs also presents the labour of mothers within the family; their daily work is described in detail as winning the praise of their husbands and children (cf. 31:10-31). The Apostle Paul was proud not to live as a burden to others, since he

worked with his own hands and assured his own livelihood (cf. *Acts* 18:3; *1 Cor* 4:12; 9:12). Paul was so convinced of the necessity of work that he laid down a strict rule for his communities: "If anyone will not work, let him not eat" (*2 Th* 3:10; cf. *1 Th* 4:11).

25. This having been said, we can appreciate the suffering created by unemployment and the lack of steady work, as reflected in the Book of Ruth, Jesus' own parable of the labourers forced to stand idly in the town square (*Mt* 20:1-16), and his personal experience of meeting people suffering from poverty and hunger. Sadly, these realities are present in many countries today, where the lack of employment opportunities takes its toll on the serenity of family life.

26. Nor can we overlook the social degeneration brought about by sin, as, for example, when human beings tyrannize nature, selfishly and even brutally ravaging it. This leads to the desertification of the earth (cf. *Gen* 3:17-19) and those social and economic imbalances denounced by the prophets, beginning with Elijah (cf. *1 Kg* 21) and culminating in Jesus' own words against injustice (cf. *Lk* 12:13; 16:1-31).

THE TENDERNESS OF AN EMBRACE

27. Christ proposed as the distinctive sign of his disciples the law of love and the gift of self for others (cf. *Mt* 22:39; *Jn* 13:34). He did so in stating a principle that fathers and mothers tend to embody in their own lives: "No one has greater love than this, to lay down one's life for one's friends" (*Jn* 15:13). Love also bears fruit in mercy and forgiveness. We see this in a particular way in the scene of the woman caught in adultery; in front of the Temple, the woman is surrounded by her accusers, but later, alone with Jesus, she meets not condemnation but the admonition to lead a more worthy life (cf. *Jn* 8:1-11).

28. Against this backdrop of love so central to the Christian experience of marriage and the family, another virtue stands out, one often overlooked in our world of frenetic and superficial relationships. It is tenderness. Let us consider the moving words of Psalm 131. As in other biblical texts (e.g., *Ex* 4:22; *Is* 49:15; *Ps* 27:10), the union between the Lord and his

faithful ones is expressed in terms of parental love. Here we see a delicate and tender intimacy between mother and child: the image is that of a babe sleeping in his mother's arms after being nursed. As the Hebrew word *gamûl* suggests, the infant is now fed and clings to his mother, who takes him to her bosom. There is a closeness that is conscious and not simply biological. Drawing on this image, the Psalmist sings: "I have calmed and quieted my soul, like a child quieted at its mother's breast" (*Ps* 131:2). We can also think of the touching words that the prophet Hosea puts on God's lips: "When Israel was a child, I loved him... I took them up in my arms... I led them with cords of compassion, with the bands of love, and I became to them as one who eases the yoke on their jaws, and I bent down to them and fed them" (*Hos* 11:1, 3-4).

29. With a gaze of faith and love, grace and fidelity, we have contemplated the relationship between human families and the divine Trinity. The word of God tells us that the family is entrusted to a man, a woman and their children, so that they may become a communion of persons in the image of the union of the Father, the Son and the Holy Spirit. Begetting and raising children, for its part, mirrors God's creative work. The family is called to join in daily prayer, to read the word of God and to share in Eucharistic communion, and thus to grow in love and become ever more fully a temple in which the Spirit dwells.

30. Every family should look to the icon of the Holy Family of Nazareth. Its daily life had its share of burdens and even nightmares, as when they met with Herod's implacable violence. This last was an experience that, sad to say, continues to afflict the many refugee families who in our day feel rejected and helpless. Like the Magi, our families are invited to contemplate the Child and his Mother, to bow down and worship him (cf. *Mt* 2:11). Like Mary, they are asked to face their family's challenges with courage and serenity, in good times and bad, and to keep in their heart the great things which God has done (cf. *Lk* 2:19, 51). The treasury of Mary's heart also contains the experiences of every family, which she cherishes. For this reason, she can help us understand the meaning of these experiences and to hear the message God wishes to communicate through the life of our families.

CHAPTER TWO

THE EXPERIENCES AND CHALLENGES OF FAMILIES

31. The welfare of the family is decisive for the future of the world and that of the Church. Countless studies have been made of marriage and the family, their current problems and challenges. We do well to focus on concrete realities, since "the call and the demands of the Spirit resound in the events of history", and through these "the Church can also be guided to a more profound understanding of the inexhaustible mystery of marriage and the family".[8] I will not attempt here to present all that might be said about the family today. Nonetheless, because the Synod Fathers examined the situation of families worldwide, I consider it fitting to take up some of their pastoral insights, along with concerns derived from my own experience.

THE CURRENT REALITY OF THE FAMILY

32. "Faithful to Christ's teaching we look to the reality of the family today in all its complexity, with both its lights and shadows… Anthropological and cultural changes in our times influence all aspects of life and call for an analytic and diversified approach".[9] Several decades ago, the Spanish bishops noted that families have come to enjoy greater freedom "through an equitable distribution of duties, responsibilities and tasks"; indeed, "a greater emphasis on personal communication between the spouses helps to make family life more humane", while "neither today's society nor that to which we are progressing allow an uncritical survival of older forms and models".[10] It is also evident that "the principal tendencies in anthropological-cultural changes" are leading "individuals, in personal and family life, to receive less and less support from social structures than in the past".[11]

---

[8] John Paul II, Apostolic Exhortation *Familiaris Consortio* (22 November 1981), 4: AAS 74 (1982), 84.

[9] *Relatio Synodi* 2014, 5.

[10] Spanish Bishops' Conference, *Matrimonio y familia* (6 July 1979), 3, 16, 23.

[11] *Relatio Finalis* 2015, 5.

33. On the other hand, "equal consideration needs to be given to the growing danger represented by an extreme individualism which weakens family bonds and ends up considering each member of the family as an isolated unit, leading in some cases to the idea that one's personality is shaped by his or her desires, which are considered absolute".[12] "The tensions created by an overly individualistic culture, caught up with possessions and pleasures, leads to intolerance and hostility in families".[13] Here I would also include today's fast pace of life, stress and the organization of society and labour, since all these are cultural factors which militate against permanent decisions. We also encounter widespread uncertainty and ambiguity. For example, we rightly value a personalism that opts for authenticity as opposed to mere conformity. While this can favour spontaneity and a better use of people's talents, if misdirected it can foster attitudes of constant suspicion, fear of commitment, self-centredness and arrogance. Freedom of choice makes it possible to plan our lives and to make the most of ourselves. Yet if this freedom lacks noble goals or personal discipline, it degenerates into an inability to give oneself generously to others. Indeed, in many countries where the number of marriages is decreasing, more and more people are choosing to live alone or simply to spend time together without cohabiting. We can also point to a praiseworthy concern for justice; but if misunderstood, this can turn citizens into clients interested solely in the provision of services.

34. When these factors affect our understanding of the family, it can come to be seen as a way station, helpful when convenient, or a setting in which rights can be asserted while relationships are left to the changing winds of personal desire and circumstances. Ultimately, it is easy nowadays to confuse genuine freedom with the idea that each individual can act arbitrarily, as if there were no truths, values and principles to provide guidance, and everything were possible and permissible. The ideal of marriage, marked by a commitment to exclusivity and stability, is swept aside whenever it proves inconvenient or tiresome. The fear of loneliness and the desire for stability and fidelity exist side by side

---

[12] *Relatio Synodi* 2014, 5.

[13] *Relatio Finalis* 2015, 8.

with a growing fear of entrapment in a relationship that could hamper the achievement of one's personal goals.

35. As Christians, we can hardly stop advocating marriage simply to avoid countering contemporary sensibilities, or out of a desire to be fashionable or a sense of helplessness in the face of human and moral failings. We would be depriving the world of values that we can and must offer. It is true that there is no sense in simply decrying present-day evils, as if this could change things. Nor it is helpful to try to impose rules by sheer authority. What we need is a more responsible and generous effort to present the reasons and motivations for choosing marriage and the family, and in this way to help men and women better to respond to the grace that God offers them.

36. We also need to be humble and realistic, acknowledging that at times the way we present our Christian beliefs and treat other people has helped contribute to today's problematic situation. We need a healthy dose of self-criticism. Then too, we often present marriage in such a way that its unitive meaning, its call to grow in love and its ideal of mutual assistance are overshadowed by an almost exclusive insistence on the duty of procreation. Nor have we always provided solid guidance to young married couples, understanding their timetables, their way of thinking and their concrete concerns. At times we have also proposed a far too abstract and almost artificial theological ideal of marriage, far removed from the concrete situations and practical possibilities of real families. This excessive idealization, especially when we have failed to inspire trust in God's grace, has not helped to make marriage more desirable and attractive, but quite the opposite.

37. We have long thought that simply by stressing doctrinal, bioethical and moral issues, without encouraging openness to grace, we were providing sufficient support to families, strengthening the marriage bond and giving meaning to marital life. We find it difficult to present marriage more as a dynamic path to personal development and fulfilment than as a lifelong burden. We also find it hard to make room for the consciences of the faithful, who very often respond as best they can to the Gospel amid

their limitations, and are capable of carrying out their own discernment in complex situations. We have been called to form consciences, not to replace them.

38. We must be grateful that most people do value family relationships that are permanent and marked by mutual respect. They appreciate the Church's efforts to offer guidance and counselling in areas related to growth in love, overcoming conflict and raising children. Many are touched by the power of grace experienced in sacramental Reconciliation and in the Eucharist, grace that helps them face the challenges of marriage and the family. In some countries, especially in various parts of Africa, secularism has not weakened certain traditional values, and marriages forge a strong bond between two wider families, with clearly defined structures for dealing with problems and conflicts. Nowadays we are grateful too for the witness of marriages that have not only proved lasting, but also fruitful and loving. All these factors can inspire a positive and welcoming pastoral approach capable of helping couples to grow in appreciation of the demands of the Gospel. Yet we have often been on the defensive, wasting pastoral energy on denouncing a decadent world without being proactive in proposing ways of finding true happiness. Many people feel that the Church's message on marriage and the family does not clearly reflect the preaching and attitudes of Jesus, who set forth a demanding ideal yet never failed to show compassion and closeness to the frailty of individuals like the Samaritan woman or the woman caught in adultery.

39. This is hardly to suggest that we cease warning against a cultural decline that fails to promote love or self-giving. The consultation that took place prior to the last two Synods pointed to the various symptoms of a "culture of the ephemeral". Here I think, for example, of the speed with which people move from one affective relationship to another. They believe, along the lines of social networks, that love can be connected or disconnected at the whim of the consumer, and the relationship quickly "blocked". I think too of the fears associated with permanent commitment, the obsession with free time, and those relationships that weigh costs and benefits for the sake of remedying loneliness, providing protection, or offering some service. We treat affective relationships

the way we treat material objects and the environment: everything is disposable; everyone uses and throws away, takes and breaks, exploits and squeezes to the last drop. Then, goodbye. Narcissism makes people incapable of looking beyond themselves, beyond their own desires and needs. Yet sooner or later, those who use others end up being used themselves, manipulated and discarded by that same mind-set. It is also worth noting that breakups often occur among older adults who seek a kind of "independence" and reject the ideal of growing old together, looking after and supporting one another.

40. "At the risk of oversimplifying, we might say that we live in a culture which pressures young people not to start a family, because they lack possibilities for the future. Yet this same culture presents others with so many options that they too are dissuaded from starting a family".[14] In some countries, many young persons "postpone a wedding for economic reasons, work or study. Some do so for other reasons, such as the influence of ideologies which devalue marriage and family, the desire to avoid the failures of other couples, the fear of something they consider too important and sacred, the social opportunities and economic benefits associated with simply living together, a purely emotional and romantic conception of love, the fear of losing their freedom and independence, and the rejection of something conceived as purely institutional and bureaucratic".[15] We need to find the right language, arguments and forms of witness that can help us reach the hearts of young people, appealing to their capacity for generosity, commitment, love and even heroism, and in this way inviting them to take up the challenge of marriage with enthusiasm and courage.

41. The Synod Fathers noted that "cultural tendencies in today's world seem to set no limits on a person's affectivity"; indeed, "a narcissistic, unstable or changeable affectivity does not always allow a person to grow to maturity". They also expressed concern about the current "spread of pornography and the commercialization of the body", fostered also

---

[14] *Address to the United States Congress* (24 September 2015): *L'Osservatore Romano*, 26 September 2015, p. 7.

[15] *Relatio Finalis* 2015, 29.

by a misuse of the internet, and about those "reprehensible situations where people are forced into prostitution". In this context, "couples are often uncertain, hesitant and struggling to find ways to grow. Many tend to remain in the early stages of their affective and sexual life. A crisis in a couple's relationship destabilizes the family and may lead, through separation and divorce, to serious consequences for adults, children and society as a whole, weakening its individual and social bonds".[16] Marital problems are "often confronted in haste and without the courage to have patience and reflect, to make sacrifices and to forgive one another. Failures give rise to new relationships, new couples, new civil unions, and new marriages, creating family situations which are complex and problematic for the Christian life".[17]

42. Furthermore, "the decline in population, due to a mentality against having children and promoted by the world politics of reproductive health, creates not only a situation in which the relationship between generations is no longer ensured but also the danger that, over time, this decline will lead to economic impoverishment and a loss of hope in the future. The development of bio-technology has also had a major impact on the birth rate".[18] Added to this are other factors such as "industrialization, the sexual revolution, the fear of overpopulation and economic problems... Consumerism may also deter people from having children, simply so they can maintain a certain freedom and life-style".[19] The upright consciences of spouses who have been generous in transmitting life may lead them, for sufficiently serious reasons, to limit the number of their children, yet precisely "for the sake of this dignity of conscience, the Church strongly rejects the forced State intervention in favour of contraception, sterilization and even abortion".[20] Such measures are unacceptable even in places with high birth rates, yet also in countries with disturbingly low birth rates we see politicians encouraging them. As the bishops of

---

[16] *Relatio Synodi* 2014, 10.

[17] THIRD EXTRAORDINARY GENERAL ASSEMBLY OF THE SYNOD OF BISHOPS, *Message*, 18 October 2014.

[18] *Relatio Synodi* 2014, 10.

[19] *Relatio Finalis* 2015, 7.

[20] *Ibid.*, 63.

Korea have said, this is "to act in a way that is self-contradictory and to neglect one's duty".[21]

43. The weakening of faith and religious practice in some societies has an effect on families, leaving them more isolated amid their difficulties. The Synod Fathers noted that "one symptom of the great poverty of contemporary culture is loneliness, arising from the absence of God in a person's life and the fragility of relationships. There is also a general feeling of powerlessness in the face of socio-cultural realities that oftentimes end up crushing families... Families often feel abandoned due to a lack of interest and attention on the part of institutions. The negative impact on the social order is clear, as seen in the demographic crisis, in the difficulty of raising children, in a hesitancy to welcome new life, in a tendency to see older persons as a burden, and in an increase of emotional problems and outbreaks of violence. The State has the responsibility to pass laws and create work to ensure the future of young people and help them realize their plan of forming a family".[22]

44. The lack of dignified or affordable housing often leads to the postponement of formal relationships. It should be kept in mind that "the family has the right to decent housing, fitting for family life and commensurate to the number of the members, in a physical environment that provides the basic services for the life of the family and the community".[23] Families and homes go together. This makes us see how important it is to insist on the rights of the family and not only those of individuals. The family is a good which society cannot do without, and it ought to be protected.[24] "The Church has always held it part of her mission to promote marriage and the family and to defend them against those who attack them",[25] especially today, when they are given scarce

---

[21] CATHOLIC BISHOPS' CONFERENCE OF KOREA, *Towards a Culture of Life!* (15 March 2007), 2.

[22] *Relatio Synodi* 2014, 6.

[23] PONTIFICAL COUNCIL FOR THE FAMILY, *Charter of the Rights of the Family* (22 October 1983), Art. 11.

[24] Cf. *Relatio Finalis* 2015, 11-12.

[25] PONTIFICAL COUNCIL FOR THE FAMILY, *Charter of the Rights of the Family* (22 October 1983), Introduction.

attention in political agendas. Families have the right to "to be able to count on an adequate family policy on the part of public authorities in the juridical, economic, social and fiscal domains".[26] At times families suffer terribly when, faced with the illness of a loved one, they lack access to adequate health care, or struggle to find dignified employment. "Economic constraints prohibit a family's access to education, cultural activities and involvement in the life of society. In many ways, the present-day economic situation is keeping people from participating in society. Families, in particular, suffer from problems related to work, where young people have few possibilities and job offers are very selective and insecure. Workdays are long and oftentimes made more burdensome by extended periods away from home. This situation does not help family members to gather together or parents to be with their children in such a way as to nurture their relationships each day".[27]

45. "A great number of children are born outside of wedlock, many of whom subsequently grow up with just one of their parents or in a blended or reconstituted family... The sexual exploitation of children is yet another scandalous and perverse reality in present-day society. Societies experiencing violence due to war, terrorism or the presence of organized crime are witnessing the deterioration of the family, above all in large cities, where, on their outskirts, the so-called phenomenon of 'street-children' is on the rise".[28] The sexual abuse of children is all the more scandalous when it occurs in places where they ought to be most safe, particularly in families, schools, communities and Christian institutions.[29]

46. "Migration is another sign of the times to be faced and understood in terms of its negative effects on family life".[30] The recent Synod drew attention to this issue, noting that "in various ways, migration affects whole populations in different parts of the world. The Church has exercised

---

[26] *Ibid.*, 9.
[27] *Relatio Finalis* 2015, 14.
[28] *Relatio Synodi* 2014, 8.
[29] Cf. *Relatio Finalis* 2015, 78.
[30] *Relatio Synodi* 2014, 8.

a major role in this area. Maintaining and expanding this witness to the Gospel (cf. *Mt* 25:35) is urgently needed today more than ever... Human mobility, which corresponds to the natural historical movement of peoples, can prove to be a genuine enrichment for both families that migrate and countries that welcome them. Furthermore, forced migration of families, resulting from situations of war, persecution, poverty and injustice, and marked by the vicissitudes of a journey that often puts lives at risk, traumatizes people and destabilizes families. In accompanying migrants, the Church needs a specific pastoral programme addressed not only to families that migrate but also to those family members who remain behind. This pastoral activity must be implemented with due respect for their cultures, for the human and religious formation from which they come and for the spiritual richness of their rites and traditions, even by means of a specific pastoral care... Migration is particularly dramatic and devastating to families and individuals when it takes place illegally and is supported by international networks of human trafficking. This is equally true when it involves women or unaccompanied children who are forced to endure long periods of time in temporary facilities and refugee camps, where it is impossible to start a process of integration. Extreme poverty and other situations of family breakdown sometimes even lead families to sell their children for prostitution or for organ trafficking".[31] "The persecution of Christians and ethnic and religious minorities in many parts of the world, especially in the Middle East, are a great trial not only for the Church but also the entire international community. Every effort should be encouraged, even in a practical way, to assist families and Christian communities to remain in their native lands".[32]

47. The Fathers also called particular attention to "families of persons with special needs, where the unexpected challenge of dealing with a disability can upset a family's equilibrium, desires and expectations... Families who lovingly accept the difficult trial of a child with special needs are greatly to be admired. They render the Church and society an invaluable

---

[31] *Relatio Finalis* 2015, 23; cf. *Message for the World Day of Migrants and Refugees* on 17 January 2016 (12 September 2015), *L'Osservatore Romano*, 2 October 2015, p. 8.

[32] *Relatio Finalis* 2015, 24.

witness of faithfulness to the gift of life. In these situations, the family can discover, together with the Christian community, new approaches, new ways of acting, a different way of understanding and identifying with others, by welcoming and caring for the mystery of the frailty of human life. People with disabilities are a gift for the family and an opportunity to grow in love, mutual aid and unity... If the family, in the light of the faith, accepts the presence of persons with special needs, they will be able to recognize and ensure the quality and value of every human life, with its proper needs, rights and opportunities. This approach will promote care and services on behalf of these disadvantaged persons and will encourage people to draw near to them and provide affection at every stage of their life".[33] Here I would stress that dedication and concern shown to migrants and to persons with special needs alike is a sign of the Spirit. Both situations are paradigmatic: they serve as a test of our commitment to show mercy in welcoming others and to help the vulnerable to be fully a part of our communities.

48. "Most families have great respect for the elderly, surrounding them with affection and considering them a blessing. A special word of appreciation is due to those associations and family movements committed to serving the elderly, both spiritually and socially... In highly industrialized societies, where the number of elderly persons is growing even as the birth rate declines, they can be regarded as a burden. On the other hand, the care that they require often puts a strain on their loved ones".[34] "Care and concern for the final stages of life is all the more necessary today, when contemporary society attempts to remove every trace of death and dying. The elderly who are vulnerable and dependent are at times unfairly exploited simply for economic advantage. Many families show us that it is possible to approach the last stages of life by emphasizing the importance of a person's sense of fulfilment and participation in the Lord's paschal mystery. A great number of elderly people are cared for in Church institutions, where, materially and spiritually, they can live in a peaceful, family atmosphere. Euthanasia and assisted suicide are serious threats to families worldwide; in many

---

[33] *Ibid.*, 21.

[34] *Ibid.*, 17.

countries, they have been legalized. The Church, while firmly opposing these practices, feels the need to assist families who take care of their elderly and infirm members".[35]

49. Here I would also like to mention the situation of families living in dire poverty and great limitations. The problems faced by poor households are often all the more trying.[36] For example, if a single mother has to raise a child by herself and needs to leave the child alone at home while she goes to work, the child can grow up exposed to all kind of risks and obstacles to personal growth. In such difficult situations of need, the Church must be particularly concerned to offer understanding, comfort and acceptance, rather than imposing straightaway a set of rules that only lead people to feel judged and abandoned by the very Mother called to show them God's mercy. Rather than offering the healing power of grace and the light of the Gospel message, some would "indoctrinate" that message, turning it into "dead stones to be hurled at others".[37]

SOME CHALLENGES

50. The responses given to the two pre-synodal consultations spoke of a great variety of situations and the new challenges that they pose. In addition to those already mentioned, many of the respondents pointed to the problems families face in raising children. In many cases, parents come home exhausted, not wanting to talk, and many families no longer even share a common meal. Distractions abound, including an addiction to television. This makes it all the more difficult for parents to hand on the faith to their children. Other responses pointed to the effect of severe stress on families, who often seem more caught up with securing their future than with enjoying the present. This is a broader cultural problem, aggravated by fears about steady employment, finances and the future of children.

---

[35] *Ibid.*, 20.

[36] Cf. *ibid.*, 15.

[37] *Concluding Address of the Fourteenth Ordinary General Assembly of the Synod of Bishops* (24 October 2015): *L'Osservatore Romano*, 26-27 October 2015, p. 13.

51. Drug use was also mentioned as one of the scourges of our time, causing immense suffering and even breakup for many families. The same is true of alcoholism, gambling and other addictions. The family could be the place where these are prevented and overcome, but society and politics fail to see that families at risk "lose the ability to act to help their members... We see the serious effects of this breakdown in families torn apart, the young uprooted and the elderly abandoned, children who are orphans of living parents, adolescents and young adults confused and unsupported."[38] As the Bishops of Mexico have pointed out, violence within families breeds new forms of social aggression, since "family relationships can also explain the tendency to a violent personality. This is often the case with families where communication is lacking, defensive attitudes predominate, the members are not supportive of one another, family activities that encourage participation are absent, the parental relationship is frequently conflictual and violent, and relationships between parents and children are marked by hostility. Violence within the family is a breeding-ground of resentment and hatred in the most basic human relationships".[39]

52. No one can think that the weakening of the family as that natural society founded on marriage will prove beneficial to society as a whole. The contrary is true: it poses a threat to the mature growth of individuals, the cultivation of community values and the moral progress of cities and countries. There is a failure to realize that only the exclusive and indissoluble union between a man and a woman has a plenary role to play in society as a stable commitment that bears fruit in new life. We need to acknowledge the great variety of family situations that can offer a certain stability, but de facto or same-sex unions, for example, may not simply be equated with marriage. No union that is temporary or closed to the transmission of life can ensure the future of society. But nowadays who is making an effort to strengthen marriages, to help married couples overcome their problems, to assist them in the work of raising children and, in general, to encourage the stability of the marriage bond?

---

[38] ARGENTINIAN BISHOPS' CONFERENCE, *Navega mar adentro* (31 May 2003), 42.

[39] MEXICAN BISHOPS' CONFERENCE, *Que en Cristo Nuestra Paz México tenga vida digna* (15 February 2009), 67.

53. "Some societies still maintain the practice of polygamy; in other places, arranged marriages are an enduring practice... In many places, not only in the West, the practice of living together before marriage is widespread, as well as a type of cohabitation which totally excludes any intention to marry".[40] In various countries, legislation facilitates a growing variety of alternatives to marriage, with the result that marriage, with its characteristics of exclusivity, indissolubility and openness to life, comes to appear as an old-fashioned and outdated option. Many countries are witnessing a legal deconstruction of the family, tending to adopt models based almost exclusively on the autonomy of the individual will. Surely it is legitimate and right to reject older forms of the traditional family marked by authoritarianism and even violence, yet this should not lead to a disparagement of marriage itself, but rather to the rediscovery of its authentic meaning and its renewal. The strength of the family "lies in its capacity to love and to teach how to love. For all a family's problems, it can always grow, beginning with love".[41]

54. In this brief overview, I would like to stress the fact that, even though significant advances have been made in the recognition of women's rights and their participation in public life, in some countries much remains to be done to promote these rights. Unacceptable customs still need to be eliminated. I think particularly of the shameful ill-treatment to which women are sometimes subjected, domestic violence and various forms of enslavement which, rather than a show of masculine power, are craven acts of cowardice. The verbal, physical, and sexual violence that women endure in some marriages contradicts the very nature of the conjugal union. I think of the reprehensible genital mutilation of women practised in some cultures, but also of their lack of equal access to dignified work and roles of decision-making. History is burdened by the excesses of patriarchal cultures that considered women inferior, yet in our own day, we cannot overlook the use of surrogate mothers and "the exploitation and commercialization of the female body in the current media culture".[42] There are those who believe that many of today's

---

[40] *Relatio Finalis* 2015, 25.

[41] *Ibid.*, 10.

[42] *Catechesis* (22 April 2015): *L'Osservatore Romano*, 23 April 2015, p. 7.

problems have arisen because of feminine emancipation. This argument, however, is not valid, "it is false, untrue, a form of male chauvinism".[43] The equal dignity of men and women makes us rejoice to see old forms of discrimination disappear, and within families there is a growing reciprocity. If certain forms of feminism have arisen which we must consider inadequate, we must nonetheless see in the women's movement the working of the Spirit for a clearer recognition of the dignity and rights of women.

55. Men "play an equally decisive role in family life, particularly with regard to the protection and support of their wives and children... Many men are conscious of the importance of their role in the family and live their masculinity accordingly. The absence of a father gravely affects family life and the upbringing of children and their integration into society. This absence, which may be physical, emotional, psychological and spiritual, deprives children of a suitable father figure".[44]

56. Yet another challenge is posed by the various forms of an ideology of gender that "denies the difference and reciprocity in nature of a man and a woman and envisages a society without sexual differences, thereby eliminating the anthropological basis of the family. This ideology leads to educational programmes and legislative enactments that promote a personal identity and emotional intimacy radically separated from the biological difference between male and female. Consequently, human identity becomes the choice of the individual, one which can also change over time".[45] It is a source of concern that some ideologies of this sort, which seek to respond to what are at times understandable aspirations, manage to assert themselves as absolute and unquestionable, even dictating how children should be raised. It needs to be emphasized that "biological sex and the socio-cultural role of sex (gender) can be distinguished but not separated".[46] On the other hand, "the technological revolution in the field of human procreation has introduced the ability to

---

[43] *Catechesis* (29 April 2015): *L'Osservatore Romano*, 30 April 2015, p. 8.

[44] *Relatio Finalis* 2015, 28.

[45] *Ibid.*, 8.

[46] *Ibid.*, 58.

manipulate the reproductive act, making it independent of the sexual relationship between a man and a woman. In this way, human life and parenthood have become modular and separable realities, subject mainly to the wishes of individuals or couples".[47] It is one thing to be understanding of human weakness and the complexities of life, and another to accept ideologies that attempt to sunder what are inseparable aspects of reality. Let us not fall into the sin of trying to replace the Creator. We are creatures, and not omnipotent. Creation is prior to us and must be received as a gift. At the same time, we are called to protect our humanity, and this means, in the first place, accepting it and respecting it as it was created.

57. I thank God that many families, which are far from considering themselves perfect, live in love, fulfil their calling and keep moving forward, even if they fall many times along the way. The Synod's reflections show us that there is no stereotype of the ideal family, but rather a challenging mosaic made up of many different realities, with all their joys, hopes and problems. The situations that concern us are challenges. We should not be trapped into wasting our energy in doleful laments, but rather seek new forms of missionary creativity. In every situation that presents itself, "the Church is conscious of the need to offer a word of truth and hope... The great values of marriage and the Christian family correspond to a yearning that is part and parcel of human existence".[48] If we see any number of problems, these should be, as the Bishops of Colombia have said, a summons to "revive our hope and to make it the source of prophetic visions, transformative actions and creative forms of charity".[49]

---

[47] *Ibid.*, 33.

[48] *Relatio Synodi* 2014, 11.

[49] COLOMBIAN BISHOPS' CONFERENCE, *A tiempos difíciles, colombianos nuevos* (13 February 2003), 3.

CHAPTER THREE

LOOKING TO JESUS:
THE VOCATION OF THE FAMILY

58. In and among families, the Gospel message should always resound; the core of that message, the kerygma, is what is "most beautiful, most excellent, most appealing and at the same time most necessary".[50] This message "has to occupy the centre of all evangelizing activity".[51] It is the first and most important proclamation, "which we must hear again and again in different ways, and which we must always announce in one form or another".[52] Indeed, "nothing is more solid, profound, secure, meaningful and wise than that message". In effect, "all Christian formation consists of entering more deeply into the kerygma".[53]

59. Our teaching on marriage and the family cannot fail to be inspired and transformed by this message of love and tenderness; otherwise, it becomes nothing more than the defence of a dry and lifeless doctrine. The mystery of the Christian family can be fully understood only in the light of the Father's infinite love revealed in Christ, who gave himself up for our sake and who continues to dwell in our midst. I now wish to turn my gaze to the living Christ, who is at the heart of so many love stories, and to invoke the fire of the Spirit upon all the world's families.

60. This brief chapter, then, will summarize the Church's teaching on marriage and the family. Here too I will mention what the Synod Fathers had to say about the light offered by our faith. They began with the gaze of Jesus and they spoke of how he "looked upon the women and men whom he met with love and tenderness, accompanying their steps in truth, patience and mercy as he proclaimed the demands of the Kingdom of

---

[50] Apostolic Exhortation *Evangelii Gaudium* (24 November 2013), 35: AAS 105 (2013), 1034.

[51] *Ibid.*, 164: AAS 105 (2013), 1088.

[52] *Ibid.*

[53] *Ibid.*, 165: AAS 105 (2013), 1089.

God".[54] The Lord is also with us today, as we seek to practise and pass on the Gospel of the family.

JESUS RESTORES AND FULFILS GOD'S PLAN

61. Contrary to those who rejected marriage as evil, the New Testament teaches that "everything created by God is good and nothing is to be rejected" (*1 Tim* 4:4). Marriage is "a gift" from the Lord (*1 Cor* 7:7). At the same time, precisely because of this positive understanding, the New Testament strongly emphasizes the need to safeguard God's gift: "Let marriage be held in honour among all, and let the marriage bed be undefiled" (*Heb* 13:4). This divine gift includes sexuality: "Do not refuse one another" (*1 Cor* 7:5).

62. The Synod Fathers noted that Jesus, "in speaking of God's original plan for man and woman, reaffirmed the indissoluble union between them, even stating that 'it was for your hardness of heart that Moses allowed you to divorce your wives, but from the beginning it was not so' (*Mt* 19:8). The indissolubility of marriage - 'what God has joined together, let no man put asunder' (*Mt* 19:6) - should not be viewed as a 'yoke' imposed on humanity, but as a 'gift' granted to those who are joined in marriage... God's indulgent love always accompanies our human journey; through grace, it heals and transforms hardened hearts, leading them back to the beginning through the way of the cross. The Gospels clearly present the example of Jesus who... proclaimed the meaning of marriage as the fulness of revelation that restores God's original plan (cf. *Mt* 19:3)".[55]

63. "Jesus, who reconciled all things in himself, restored marriage and the family to their original form (cf. *Mt* 10:1-12). Marriage and the family have been redeemed by Christ (cf. *Eph* 5:21-32) and restored in the image of the Holy Trinity, the mystery from which all true love flows. The spousal covenant, originating in creation and revealed in the history of salvation, takes on its full meaning in Christ and his Church.

---

[54] *Relatio Synodi* 2014, 12.

[55] *Ibid.*, 14.

Through his Church, Christ bestows on marriage and the family the grace necessary to bear witness to the love of God and to live the life of communion. The Gospel of the family spans the history of the world, from the creation of man and woman in the image and likeness of God (cf. *Gen* 1:26-27), to the fulfilment of the mystery of the covenant in Christ at the end of time with the marriage of the Lamb (cf. *Rev* 19:9)".[56]

64. "The example of Jesus is a paradigm for the Church... He began his public ministry with the miracle at the wedding feast of Cana (cf. *Jn* 2:1-11). He shared in everyday moments of friendship with the family of Lazarus and his sisters (cf. *Lk* 10:38) and with the family of Peter (cf. *Mk* 8:14). He sympathized with grieving parents and restored their children to life (cf. *Mk* 5:41; *Lk* 7:14-15). In this way he demonstrated the true meaning of mercy, which entails the restoration of the covenant (cf. John Paul II, *Dives in Misericordia*, 4). This is clear from his conversations with the Samaritan woman (cf. *Jn* 1:4-30) and with the woman found in adultery (cf. *Jn* 8:1-11), where the consciousness of sin is awakened by an encounter with Jesus' gratuitous love".[57]

65. The incarnation of the Word in a human family, in Nazareth, by its very newness changed the history of the world. We need to enter into the mystery of Jesus' birth, into that "yes" given by Mary to the message of the angel, when the Word was conceived in her womb, as well as the "yes" of Joseph, who gave a name to Jesus and watched over Mary. We need to contemplate the joy of the shepherds before the manger, the adoration of the Magi and the flight into Egypt, in which Jesus shares his people's experience of exile, persecution and humiliation. We need to contemplate the religious expectation of Zechariah and his joy at the birth of John the Baptist, the fulfilment of the promise made known to Simeon and Anna in the Temple and the marvel of the teachers of the Law who listened to the wisdom of the child Jesus. We then need to peer into those thirty long years when Jesus earned his keep by the work of his hands, reciting the traditional prayers and expressions of his people's faith and coming to know that ancestral faith until he made it bear fruit in the mystery of the

---

[56] *Ibid.*, 16.
[57] *Relatio Finalis* 2015, 41.

Kingdom. This is the mystery of Christmas and the secret of Nazareth, exuding the beauty of family life! It was this that so fascinated Francis of Assisi, Thérèse of the Child Jesus and Charles de Foucauld, and continues to fill Christian families with hope and joy.

66. "The covenant of love and fidelity lived by the Holy Family of Nazareth illuminates the principle which gives shape to every family, and enables it better to face the vicissitudes of life and history. On this basis, every family, despite its weaknesses, can become a light in the darkness of the world. 'Nazareth teaches us the meaning of family life, its loving communion, its simple and austere beauty, its sacred and inviolable character. May it teach how sweet and irreplaceable is its training, how fundamental and incomparable its role in the social order' (Paul VI, *Address in Nazareth*, 5 January 1964)".[58]

THE FAMILY IN THE DOCUMENTS OF THE CHURCH

67. The Second Vatican Council, in its Pastoral Constitution *Gaudium et Spes*, was concerned "to promote the dignity of marriage and the family (cf. Nos. 47-52)". The Constitution "defined marriage as a community of life and love (cf. 48), placing love at the centre of the family... 'True love between husband and wife' (49) involves mutual self-giving, includes and integrates the sexual and affective dimensions, in accordance with God's plan (cf. 48-49)". The conciliar document also emphasizes "the grounding of the spouses in Christ. Christ the Lord 'makes himself present to the Christian spouses in the sacrament of marriage' (48) and remains with them. In the incarnation, he assumes human love, purifies it and brings it to fulfilment. By his Spirit, he gives spouses the capacity to live that love, permeating every part of their lives of faith, hope and charity. In this way, the spouses are consecrated and by means of a special grace build up the Body of Christ and form a domestic church (cf. *Lumen Gentium*, 11), so that the Church, in order fully to understand her mystery, looks to the Christian family, which manifests her in a real way".[59]

---

[58] *Ibid.*, 38.
[59] *Relatio Synodi* 2014, 17.

68. "Blessed Paul VI, in the wake of the Second Vatican Council, further developed the Church's teaching on marriage and the family. In a particular way, with the Encyclical *Humanae Vitae* he brought out the intrinsic bond between conjugal love and the generation of life: 'Married love requires of husband and wife the full awareness of their obligations in the matter of responsible parenthood, which today, rightly enough, is much insisted upon, but which at the same time must be rightly understood... The exercise of responsible parenthood requires that husband and wife, keeping a right order of priorities, recognize their own duties towards God, themselves, their families and human society' (No. 10). In the Apostolic Exhortation *Evangelii Nuntiandi*, Paul VI highlighted the relationship between the family and the Church".[60]

69. "Saint John Paul II devoted special attention to the family in his catecheses on human love, in his Letter to Families *Gratissimam Sane* and particularly in his Apostolic Exhortation *Familiaris Consortio*. In these documents, the Pope defined the family as 'the way of the Church'. He also offered a general vision of the vocation of men and women to love, and proposed basic guidelines for the pastoral care of the family and for the role of the family in society. In particular, by treating conjugal love (cf. No. 13), he described how spouses, in their mutual love, receive the gift of the Spirit of Christ and live their call to holiness".[61]

70. "Pope Benedict XVI, in his Encyclical *Deus Caritas Est*, returned to the topic of the truth of the love of man and woman, which is fully illuminated only in the love of the crucified Christ (cf. No. 2). He stressed that 'marriage based on an exclusive and definitive love becomes an icon of the relationship between God and his people, and vice versa. God's way of loving becomes the measure of human love' (11). Moreover, in the Encyclical *Caritas in Veritate*, he highlighted the importance of love as a principle of life in society (cf. 44), a place where we learn the experience of the common good".[62]

---

[60] *Relatio Finalis* 2015, 43.

[61] *Relatio Synodi* 2014, 18.

[62] *Ibid., 19.*

THE SACRAMENT OF MATRIMONY

71. "Scripture and Tradition give us access to a knowledge of the Trinity, which is revealed with the features of a family. The family is the image of God, who is a communion of persons. At Christ's baptism, the Father's voice was heard, calling Jesus his beloved Son, and in this love we can recognize the Holy Spirit (cf. *Mk* 1:10-11). Jesus, who reconciled all things in himself and redeemed us from sin, not only returned marriage and the family to their original form, but also raised marriage to the sacramental sign of his love for the Church (cf. *Mt* 19:1-12; *Mk* 10:1-12; *Eph* 5:21-32). In the human family, gathered by Christ, 'the image and likeness' of the Most Holy Trinity (cf. *Gen* 1:26) has been restored, the mystery from which all true love flows. Through the Church, marriage and the family receive the grace of the Holy Spirit from Christ, in order to bear witness to the Gospel of God's love".[63]

72. The sacrament of marriage is not a social convention, an empty ritual or merely the outward sign of a commitment. The sacrament is a gift given for the sanctification and salvation of the spouses, since "their mutual belonging is a real representation, through the sacramental sign, of the same relationship between Christ and the Church. The married couple are therefore a permanent reminder for the Church of what took place on the cross; they are for one another and for their children witnesses of the salvation in which they share through the sacrament".[64] Marriage is a vocation, inasmuch as it is a response to a specific call to experience conjugal love as an imperfect sign of the love between Christ and the Church. Consequently, the decision to marry and to have a family ought to be the fruit of a process of vocational discernment.

73. "Mutual self-giving in the sacrament of matrimony is grounded in the grace of baptism, which establishes the foundational covenant of every person with Christ in the Church. In accepting each other, and with Christ's grace, the engaged couple promise each other total self-giving, faithfulness and openness to new life. The couple recognizes

---

[63] *Relatio Finalis* 2015, 38.

[64] JOHN PAUL II, Apostolic Exhortation *Familiaris Consortio* (22 November 1981), 13: AAS 74 (1982), 94.

these elements as constitutive of marriage, gifts offered to them by God, and take seriously their mutual commitment, in God's name and in the presence of the Church. Faith thus makes it possible for them to assume the goods of marriage as commitments that can be better kept through the help of the grace of the sacrament... Consequently, the Church looks to married couples as the heart of the entire family, which, in turn, looks to Jesus".[65] The sacrament is not a "thing" or a "power", for in it Christ himself "now encounters Christian spouses... He dwells with them, gives them the strength to take up their crosses and so follow him, to rise again after they have fallen, to forgive one another, to bear one another's burdens".[66] Christian marriage is a sign of how much Christ loved his Church in the covenant sealed on the cross, yet it also makes that love present in the communion of the spouses. By becoming one flesh, they embody the espousal of our human nature by the Son of God. That is why "in the joys of their love and family life, he gives them here on earth a foretaste of the wedding feast of the Lamb".[67] Even though the analogy between the human couple of husband and wife, and that of Christ and his Church, is "imperfect",[68] it inspires us to beg the Lord to bestow on every married couple an outpouring of his divine love.

74. Sexual union, lovingly experienced and sanctified by the sacrament, is in turn a path of growth in the life of grace for the couple. It is the "nuptial mystery".[69] The meaning and value of their physical union is expressed in the words of consent, in which they accepted and offered themselves each to the other, in order to share their lives completely. Those words give meaning to the sexual relationship and free it from ambiguity. More generally, the common life of husband and wife, the entire network of relations that they build with their children and the world around them, will be steeped in and strengthened by the grace of the sacrament. For the sacrament of marriage flows from the incarnation

---

[65] *Relatio Synodi* 2014, 21.

[66] *Catechism of the Catholic Church*, 1642.

[67] *Ibid.*

[68] *Catechesis* (6 May 2015): *L'Osservatore Romano*, 7 May 2015, p. 8.

[69] Leo the Great, *Epistula Rustico Narbonensi Episcopo*, Inquis. IV: PL 54, 1205A; cf. Hincmar of Rheims, *Epist.* 22: PL 126, 142.

and the paschal mystery, whereby God showed the fulness of his love for humanity by becoming one with us. Neither of the spouses will be alone in facing whatever challenges may come their way. Both are called to respond to God's gift with commitment, creativity, perseverance and daily effort. They can always invoke the assistance of the Holy Spirit who consecrated their union, so that his grace may be felt in every new situation that they encounter.

75. In the Church's Latin tradition, the ministers of the sacrament of marriage are the man and the woman who marry;[70] by manifesting their consent and expressing it physically, they receive a great gift. Their consent and their bodily union are the divinely appointed means whereby they become "one flesh". By their baptismal consecration, they were enabled to join in marriage as the Lord's ministers and thus to respond to God's call. Hence, when two non-Christian spouses receive baptism, they need not renew their marriage vows; they need simply not reject them, since by the reception of baptism their union automatically becomes sacramental. Canon Law also recognizes the validity of certain unions celebrated without the presence of an ordained minister.[71] The natural order has been so imbued with the redemptive grace of Jesus that "a valid matrimonial contract cannot exist between the baptized without it being by that fact a sacrament".[72] The Church can require that the wedding be celebrated publicly, with the presence of witnesses and other conditions that have varied over the course of time, but this does not detract from the fact that the couple who marry are the ministers of the sacrament. Nor does it affect the centrality of the consent given by the man and the woman, which of itself establishes the sacramental bond. This having been said, there is a need for further reflection on God's action in the marriage rite; this is clearly manifested in the Oriental Churches through the importance of the blessing that the couple receive as a sign of the gift of the Spirit.

---

[70] Cf. PIUS XII, Encyclical Letter *Mystici Corporis Christi* (29 June 1943): AAS 35 (1943), 202: *"Matrimonio enim quo coniuges sibi invicem sunt ministri gratiae ..."*

[71] Cf. *Code of Canon Law*, cc. 1116; 1161-1165; *Code of Canons of the Eastern Churches*, 832; 848-852.

[72] *Ibid.*, c. 1055 §2.

SEEDS OF THE WORD AND IMPERFECT SITUATIONS

76. "The Gospel of the family also nourishes seeds that are still waiting to grow, and serves as the basis for caring for those plants that are wilting and must not be neglected."[73] Thus, building on the gift of Christ in the sacrament, married couples "may be led patiently further on in order to achieve a deeper grasp and a fuller integration of this mystery in their lives".[74]

77. Appealing to the Bible's teaching that all was created through Christ and for Christ (cf. *Col* 1:16), the Synod Fathers noted that "the order of redemption illuminates and fulfils that of creation. Natural marriage, therefore, is fully understood in the light of its fulfilment in the sacrament of Matrimony: only in contemplating Christ does a person come to know the deepest truth about human relationships. 'Only in the mystery of the Incarnate Word does the mystery of man take on light... Christ, the new Adam, by the revelation of the mystery of the Father and his love, fully reveals man to himself and makes his supreme calling clear' (*Gaudium et Spes*, 22). It is particularly helpful to understand in a Christocentric key... the good of the spouses (*bonum coniugum*)",[75] which includes unity, openness to life, fidelity, indissolubility and, within Christian marriage, mutual support on the path towards complete friendship with the Lord. "Discernment of the presence of 'seeds of the Word' in other cultures (cf. *Ad Gentes* 11) can also apply to the reality of marriage and the family. In addition to true natural marriage, positive elements exist in the forms of marriage found in other religious traditions",[76] even if, at times, obscurely. We can readily say that "anyone who wants to bring into this world a family which teaches children to be excited by every gesture aimed at overcoming evil - a family which shows that the Spirit is alive and at work - will encounter our gratitude and our appreciation. Whatever the people, religion or region to which they belong!"[77]

---

[73] *Relatio Synodi* 2014, 23.

[74] JOHN PAUL II, Apostolic Exhortation *Familiaris Consortio* (22 November 1981), 9: AAS 74 (1982), 90.

[75] *Relatio Finalis* 2015, 47.

[76] *Ibid.*

[77] *Homily for the Concluding Mass of the Eighth World Meeting of Families in Philadelphia* (27 September 2015): *L'Osservatore Romano*, 28-29 September 2015, p. 7.

78. "The light of Christ enlightens every person (cf. *Jn* 1:9; *Gaudium et Spes*, 22). Seeing things with the eyes of Christ inspires the Church's pastoral care for the faithful who are living together, or are only married civilly, or are divorced and remarried. Following this divine pedagogy, the Church turns with love to those who participate in her life in an imperfect manner: she seeks the grace of conversion for them; she encourages them to do good, to take loving care of each other and to serve the community in which they live and work... When a couple in an irregular union attains a noteworthy stability through a public bond - and is characterized by deep affection, responsibility towards the children and the ability to overcome trials - this can be seen as an opportunity, where possible, to lead them to celebrate the sacrament of Matrimony".[78]

79. "When faced with difficult situations and wounded families, it is always necessary to recall this general principle: 'Pastors must know that, for the sake of truth, they are obliged to exercise careful discernment of situations' (*Familiaris Consortio*, 84). The degree of responsibility is not equal in all cases and factors may exist which limit the ability to make a decision. Therefore, while clearly stating the Church's teaching, pastors are to avoid judgements that do not take into account the complexity of various situations, and they are to be attentive, by necessity, to how people experience and endure distress because of their condition".[79]

THE TRANSMISSION OF LIFE AND THE REARING OF CHILDREN

80. Marriage is firstly an "intimate partnership of life and love"[80] which is a good for the spouses themselves,[81] while sexuality is "ordered to the conjugal love of man and woman".[82] It follows that "spouses to whom God has not granted children can have a conjugal life full

---

[78] *Relatio Finalis* 2015, 53-54.

[79] *Ibid.*, 51.

[80] SECOND VATICAN ECUMENICAL COUNCIL, Pastoral Constitution on the Church in the Modern World *Gaudium et Spes*, 48.

[81] Cf. *Code of Canon Law*, c. 1055 § 1: "*ad bonum coniugum atque ad prolis generationem et educationem ordinatum*".

[82] *Catechism of the Catholic Church*, 2360.

of meaning, in both human and Christian terms".[83] Nonetheless, the conjugal union is ordered to procreation "by its very nature".[84] The child who is born "does not come from outside as something added on to the mutual love of the spouses, but springs from the very heart of that mutual giving, as its fruit and fulfilment".[85] He or she does not appear at the end of a process, but is present from the beginning of love as an essential feature, one that cannot be denied without disfiguring that love itself. From the outset, love refuses every impulse to close in on itself; it is open to a fruitfulness that draws it beyond itself. Hence no genital act of husband and wife can refuse this meaning,[86] even when for various reasons it may not always in fact beget a new life.

81. A child deserves to be born of that love, and not by any other means, for "he or she is not something owed to one, but is a gift",[87] which is "the fruit of the specific act of the conjugal love of the parents".[88] This is the case because, "according to the order of creation, conjugal love between a man and a woman, and the transmission of life are ordered to each other (cf. *Gen* 1:27-28). Thus the Creator made man and woman share in the work of his creation and, at the same time, made them instruments of his love, entrusting to them the responsibility for the future of mankind, through the transmission of human life".[89]

82. The Synod Fathers stated that "the growth of a mentality that would reduce the generation of human life to one variable of an individual's or a couple's plans is clearly evident".[90] The Church's teaching is meant to "help couples to experience in a complete, harmonious and

---

[83] *Ibid.*, 1654.

[84] SECOND VATICAN ECUMENICAL COUNCIL, Pastoral Constitution on the Church in the Modern World *Gaudium et Spes*, 48.

[85] *Catechism of the Catholic Church*, 2366.

[86] Cf. PAUL VI, Encyclical Letter *Humanae Vitae* (25 July 1968), 11-12: AAS 60 (1968), 488-489.

[87] *Catechism of the Catholic Church*, 2378.

[88] CONGREGATION FOR THE DOCTRINE OF THE FAITH, Instruction *Donum Vitae* (22 February 1987), II, 8: AAS 80 (1988), 97.

[89] *Relatio Finalis* 2015, 63.

[90] *Relatio Synodi* 2014, 57.

conscious way their communion as husband and wife, together with their responsibility for procreating life. We need to return to the message of the Encyclical *Humanae Vitae* of Blessed Pope Paul VI, which highlights the need to respect the dignity of the person in morally assessing methods of regulating birth... The choice of adoption or foster parenting can also express that fruitfulness which is a characteristic of married life".[91] With special gratitude the Church "supports families who accept, raise and surround with affection children with various disabilities".[92]

83. Here I feel it urgent to state that, if the family is the sanctuary of life, the place where life is conceived and cared for, it is a horrendous contradiction when it becomes a place where life is rejected and destroyed. So great is the value of a human life, and so inalienable the right to life of an innocent child growing in the mother's womb, that no alleged right to one's own body can justify a decision to terminate that life, which is an end in itself and which can never be considered the "property" of another human being. The family protects human life in all its stages, including its last. Consequently, "those who work in healthcare facilities are reminded of the moral duty of conscientious objection. Similarly, the Church not only feels the urgency to assert the right to a natural death, without aggressive treatment and euthanasia", but likewise "firmly rejects the death penalty".[93]

84. The Synod Fathers also wished to emphasize that "one of the fundamental challenges facing families today is undoubtedly that of raising children, made all the more difficult and complex by today's cultural reality and the powerful influence of the media".[94] "The Church assumes a valuable role in supporting families, starting with Christian initiation, through welcoming communities".[95] At the same time I feel it important to reiterate that the overall education of children is a "most serious duty"

---

[91] *Ibid.*, 58.

[92] *Ibid.*, 57.

[93] *Relatio Finalis* 2015, 64.

[94] *Relatio Synodi* 2014, 60.

[95] *Ibid.*, 61.

and at the same time a "primary right" of parents.[96] This is not just a task or a burden, but an essential and inalienable right that parents are called to defend and of which no one may claim to deprive them. The State offers educational programmes in a subsidiary way, supporting the parents in their indeclinable role; parents themselves enjoy the right to choose freely the kind of education - accessible and of good quality - which they wish to give their children in accordance with their convictions. Schools do not replace parents, but complement them. This is a basic principle: "all other participants in the process of education are only able to carry out their responsibilities in the name of the parents, with their consent and, to a certain degree, with their authorization".[97] Still, "a rift has opened up between the family and society, between family and the school; the educational pact today has been broken and thus the educational alliance between society and the family is in crisis".[98]

85. The Church is called to co-operate with parents through suitable pastoral initiatives, assisting them in the fulfilment of their educational mission. She must always do this by helping them to appreciate their proper role and to realize that by their reception of the sacrament of marriage they become ministers of their children's education. In educating them, they build up the Church,[99] and in so doing, they accept a God-given vocation.[100]

THE FAMILY AND THE CHURCH

86. "With inner joy and deep comfort, the Church looks to the families who remain faithful to the teachings of the Gospel, encouraging them and thanking them for the testimony they offer. For they bear witness, in a credible way, to the beauty of marriage as indissoluble and perpetually faithful. Within the family 'which could be called a domestic church'

---

[96] *Code of Canon Law*, c. 1136; cf. *Code of Canons of the Eastern Churches*, 627.

[97] PONTIFICAL COUNCIL FOR THE FAMILY, *The Truth and Meaning of Human Sexuality* (8 December 1995), 23.

[98] *Catechesis* (20 May 2015): *L'Osservatore Romano*, 21 May 2015, p. 8.

[99] JOHN PAUL II, Apostolic Exhortation *Familiaris Consortio* (28 November 1981) 38: AAS 74 (1982), 129.

[100] Cf. *Address to the Diocesan Conference of Rome* (14 June 2015): *L'Osservatore Romano*, 15-16 June 2015, p. 8.

(*Lumen Gentium*, 11), individuals enter upon an ecclesial experience of communion among persons, which reflects, through grace, the mystery of the Holy Trinity. 'Here one learns endurance and the joy of work, fraternal love, generous - even repeated - forgiveness, and above all divine worship in prayer and the offering of one's life' (*Catechism of the Catholic Church*, 1657)".[101]

87. The Church is a family of families, constantly enriched by the lives of all those domestic churches. "In virtue of the sacrament of matrimony, every family becomes, in effect, a good for the Church. From this standpoint, reflecting on the interplay between the family and the Church will prove a precious gift for the Church in our time. The Church is good for the family, and the family is good for the Church. The safeguarding of the Lord's gift in the sacrament of matrimony is a concern not only of individual families but of the entire Christian community".[102]

88. The experience of love in families is a perennial source of strength for the life of the Church. "The unitive end of marriage is a constant summons to make this love grow and deepen. Through their union in love, the couple experiences the beauty of fatherhood and motherhood, and shares plans, trials, expectations and concerns; they learn care for one another and mutual forgiveness. In this love, they celebrate their happy moments and support each other in the difficult passages of their life together... The beauty of this mutual, gratuitous gift, the joy which comes from a life that is born and the loving care of all family members - from toddlers to the elderly - are just a few of the fruits which make the response to the vocation of the family unique and irreplaceable",[103] both for the Church and for society as a whole.

---

[101] *Relatio Synodi* 2014, 23.
[102] *Relatio Finalis* 2015, 52.
[103] *Ibid.*, 49-50.

CHAPTER FOUR
LOVE IN MARRIAGE

89. All that has been said so far would be insufficient to express the Gospel of marriage and the family, were we not also to *speak of love*. For we cannot encourage a path of fidelity and mutual self-giving without encouraging the growth, strengthening and deepening of conjugal and family love. Indeed, the grace of the sacrament of marriage is intended before all else "to perfect the couple's love".[104] Here too we can say that, "even if I have faith so as to remove mountains, but have not love, I am nothing. If I give all I have, and if I deliver my body to be burned, but have not love, I gain nothing" (*1 Cor* 13:2-3). The word "love", however, is commonly used and often misused.[105]

OUR DAILY LOVE

90. In a lyrical passage of Saint Paul, we see some of the features of true love:

> Love is patient,
> love is kind;
> love is not jealous or boastful;
> it is not arrogant or rude.
> Love does not insist on its own way,
> it is not irritable or resentful;
> it does not rejoice at wrong,
> but rejoices in the right.
> Love bears all things,
> believes all things,
> hopes all things,
> endures all things
> (*1 Cor* 13:4-7).

---

[104] *Catechism of the Catholic Church*, 1641.

[105] Cf. BENEDICT XVI, Encyclical Letter *Deus Caritas Est* (25 December 2005), 2: AAS 98 (2006), 218.

Love is experienced and nurtured in the daily life of couples and their children. It is helpful to think more deeply about the meaning of this Pauline text and its relevance for the concrete situation of every family.

Love is patient

91. The first word used is *makrothýmei*. This does not simply have to do with "enduring all things", because we find that idea expressed at the end of the seventh verse. Its meaning is clarified by the Greek translation of the Old Testament, where we read that God is "slow to anger" (*Ex* 34:6; *Num* 14:18). It refers, then, to the quality of one who does not act on impulse and avoids giving offence. We find this quality in the God of the Covenant, who calls us to imitate him also within the life of the family. Saint Paul's texts using this word need to be read in the light of the Book of Wisdom (cf. 11:23; 12:2, 15-18), which extols God's restraint, as leaving open the possibility of repentance, yet insists on his power, as revealed in his acts of mercy. God's "patience", shown in his mercy towards sinners, is a sign of his real power.

92. Being patient does not mean letting ourselves be constantly mistreated, tolerating physical aggression or allowing other people to use us. We encounter problems whenever we think that relationships or people ought to be perfect, or when we put ourselves at the centre and expect things to turn out our way. Then everything makes us impatient, everything makes us react aggressively. Unless we cultivate patience, we will always find excuses for responding angrily. We will end up incapable of living together, antisocial, unable to control our impulses, and our families will become battlegrounds. That is why the word of God tells us: "Let all bitterness and wrath and anger and clamour and slander be put away from you, with all malice" (*Eph* 4:31). Patience takes root when I recognize that other people also have a right to live in this world, just as they are. It does not matter if they hold me back, if they unsettle my plans, or annoy me by the way they act or think, or if they are not everything I want them to be. Love always has an aspect of deep compassion that leads to accepting the other person as part of this world, even when he or she acts differently from how I would like.

Love is at the service of others

93. The next word that Paul uses is *chrestéuetai*. The word is used only here in the entire Bible. It is derived from *chrestós*: a good person, one who shows his goodness by his deeds. Here, in strict parallelism with the preceding verb, it serves as a complement. Paul wants to make it clear that "patience" is not a completely passive attitude, but one accompanied by activity, by a dynamic and creative interaction with others. The word indicates that love benefits and helps others. For this reason it is translated as "kind"; love is ever ready to be of assistance.

94. Throughout the text, it is clear that Paul wants to stress that love is more than a mere feeling. Rather, it should be understood along the lines of the Hebrew verb "to love"; it is "to do good". As Saint Ignatius of Loyola said, "Love is shown more by deeds than by words".[106] It thus shows its fruitfulness and allows us to experience the happiness of giving, the nobility and grandeur of spending ourselves unstintingly, without asking to be repaid, purely for the pleasure of giving and serving.

Love is not jealous

95. Saint Paul goes on to reject as contrary to love an attitude expressed by the verb *zelói* - to be jealous or envious. This means that love has no room for discomfiture at another person's good fortune (cf. *Acts* 7:9; 17:5). Envy is a form of sadness provoked by another's prosperity; it shows that we are not concerned for the happiness of others but only with our own well-being. Whereas love makes us rise above ourselves, envy closes us in on ourselves. True love values the other person's achievements. It does not see him or her as a threat. It frees us from the sour taste of envy. It recognizes that everyone has different gifts and a unique path in life. So it strives to discover its own road to happiness, while allowing others to find theirs.

96. In a word, love means fulfilling the last two commandments of God's Law: "You shall not covet your neighbour's house; you shall not covet your neighbour's wife, or his manservant, or his maidservant, or his ox, or his donkey, or anything that is your neighbour's" (*Ex* 20:17). Love inspires a

---

[106] *Spiritual Exercises,* Contemplation to Attain Love (230).

sincere esteem for every human being and the recognition of his or her own right to happiness. I love this person, and I see him or her with the eyes of God, who gives us everything "for our enjoyment" (*1 Tim* 6:17). As a result, I feel a deep sense of happiness and peace. This same deeply rooted love also leads me to reject the injustice whereby some possess too much and others too little. It moves me to find ways of helping society's outcasts to find a modicum of joy. That is not envy, but the desire for equality.

Love is not boastful

97. The following word, *perpereúetai*, denotes vainglory, the need to be haughty, pedantic and somewhat pushy. Those who love not only refrain from speaking too much about themselves, but are focused on others; they do not need to be the centre of attention. The word that comes next - *physioútai* - is similar, indicating that love is not arrogant. Literally, it means that we do not become "puffed up" before others. It also points to something more subtle: an obsession with showing off and a loss of a sense of reality. Such people think that, because they are more "spiritual" or "wise", they are more important than they really are. Paul uses this verb on other occasions, as when he says that "knowledge puffs up", whereas "love builds up" (*1 Cor* 8:1). Some think that they are important because they are more knowledgeable than others; they want to lord it over them. Yet what really makes us important is a love that understands, shows concern, and embraces the weak. Elsewhere the word is used to criticize those who are "inflated" with their own importance (cf. *1 Cor* 4:18) but in fact are filled more with empty words than the real "power" of the Spirit (cf. *1 Cor* 4:19).

98. It is important for Christians to show their love by the way they treat family members who are less knowledgeable about the faith, weak or less sure in their convictions. At times the opposite occurs: the supposedly mature believers within the family become unbearably arrogant. Love, on the other hand, is marked by humility; if we are to understand, forgive and serve others from the heart, our pride has to be healed and our humility must increase. Jesus told his disciples that in a world where power prevails, each tries to dominate the other, but "it shall not be so among you" (*Mt* 20:26). The inner logic of Christian love is not about

51

importance and power; rather, "whoever would be first among you must be your slave" (*Mt* 20:27). In family life, the logic of domination and competition about who is the most intelligent or powerful destroys love. Saint Peter's admonition also applies to the family: "Clothe yourselves, all of you, with humility towards one another, for 'God opposes the proud, but gives grace to the humble'" (*1 Pet* 5:5).

Love is not rude

99. To love is also to be gentle and thoughtful, and this is conveyed by the next word, *aschemonéi*. It indicates that love is not rude or impolite; it is not harsh. Its actions, words and gestures are pleasing and not abrasive or rigid. Love abhors making others suffer. Courtesy "is a school of sensitivity and disinterestedness" which requires a person "to develop his or her mind and feelings, learning how to listen, to speak and, at certain times, to keep quiet".[107] It is not something that a Christian may accept or reject. As an essential requirement of love, "every human being is bound to live agreeably with those around him".[108] Every day, "entering into the life of another, even when that person already has a part to play in our life, demands the sensitivity and restraint which can renew trust and respect. Indeed, the deeper love is, the more it calls for respect for the other's freedom and the ability to wait until the other opens the door to his or her heart".[109]

100. To be open to a genuine encounter with others, "a kind look" is essential. This is incompatible with a negative attitude that readily points out other people's shortcomings while overlooking one's own. A kind look helps us to see beyond our own limitations, to be patient and to co-operate with others, despite our differences. Loving kindness builds bonds, cultivates relationships, creates new networks of integration and knits a firm social fabric. In this way, it grows ever stronger, for without a sense of belonging we cannot sustain a commitment to others; we end up seeking our convenience alone and life in common

---

[107] OCTAVIO PAZ, *La llama doble*, Barcelona, 1993, 35.

[108] THOMAS AQUINAS, *Summa Theologiae* II-II, q. 114, art. 2, ad 1.

[109] *Catechesis* (13 May 2005): *L'Osservatore Romano*, 14 May 2015, p. 8.

becomes impossible. Antisocial persons think that others exist only for the satisfaction of their own needs. Consequently, there is no room for the gentleness of love and its expression. Those who love are capable of speaking words of comfort, strength, consolation, and encouragement. These were the words that Jesus himself spoke: "Take heart, my son!" (*Mt* 9:2); "Great is your faith!" (*Mt* 15:28); "Arise!" (*Mk* 5:41); "Go in peace" (*Lk* 7:50); "Be not afraid" (*Mt* 14:27). These are not words that demean, sadden, anger or show scorn. In our families, we must learn to imitate Jesus' own gentleness in our way of speaking to one another.

Love is generous

101. We have repeatedly said that to love another we must first love ourselves. Paul's hymn to love, however, states that love "does not seek its own interest", nor "seek what is its own". This same idea is expressed in another text: "Let each of you look not only to his own interests, but also to the interests of others" (*Phil* 2:4). The Bible makes it clear that generously serving others is far more noble than loving ourselves. Loving ourselves is only important as a psychological prerequisite for being able to love others: "If a man is mean to himself, to whom will he be generous? No one is meaner than the man who is grudging to himself" (*Sir* 14:5-6).

102. Saint Thomas Aquinas explains that "it is more proper to charity to desire to love than to desire to be loved";[110] indeed, "mothers, who are those who love the most, seek to love more than to be loved".[111] Consequently, love can transcend and overflow the demands of justice, "expecting nothing in return" (*Lk* 6:35), and the greatest of loves can lead to "laying down one's life" for another (cf. *Jn* 15:13). Can such generosity, which enables us to give freely and fully, really be possible? Yes, because it is demanded by the Gospel: "You received without pay, give without pay" (*Mt* 10:8).

Love is not irritable or resentful

103. If the first word of Paul's hymn spoke of the need for a patience that does not immediately react harshly to the weaknesses and faults

---

[110] THOMAS AQUINAS, *Summa Theologiae*, II-II, q. 27, art. 1, ad 2.

[111] *Ibid.*, q. 27, art. 1.

of others, the word he uses next - *paroxýnetai* - has to do more with an interior indignation provoked by something from without. It refers to a violent reaction within, a hidden irritation that sets us on edge where others are concerned, as if they were troublesome or threatening and thus to be avoided. To nurture such interior hostility helps no one. It only causes hurt and alienation. Indignation is only healthy when it makes us react to a grave injustice; when it permeates our attitude towards others it is harmful.

104. The Gospel tells us to look to the log in our own eye (cf. *Mt* 7:5). Christians cannot ignore the persistent admonition of God's word not to nurture anger: "Do not be overcome by evil" (*Rm* 12:21). "Let us not grow weary in doing good" (*Gal* 6:9). It is one thing to sense a sudden surge of hostility and another to give into it, letting it take root in our hearts: "Be angry but do not sin; do not let the sun go down on your anger" (*Eph* 4:26). My advice is never to let the day end without making peace in the family. "And how am I going to make peace? By getting down on my knees? No! Just by a small gesture, a little something, and harmony within your family will be restored. Just a little caress, no words are necessary. But do not let the day end without making peace in your family".[112] Our first reaction when we are annoyed should be one of heartfelt blessing, asking God to bless, free and heal that person. "On the contrary bless, for to this you have been called, that you may obtain a blessing" (*1 Pet* 3:9). If we must fight evil, so be it; but we must always say "no" to violence in the home.

Love forgives

105. Once we allow ill will to take root in our hearts, it leads to deep resentment. The phrase *ou logízetai to kakón* means that love "takes no account of evil"; "it is not resentful". The opposite of resentment is forgiveness, which is rooted in a positive attitude that seeks to understand other people's weaknesses and to excuse them. As Jesus said, "Father, forgive them; for they know not what they do" (*Lk* 23:34). Yet we keep looking for more and more faults, imagining greater evils, presuming

---

[112] *Catechesis* (13 May 2015): *L'Osservatore Romano*, 14 May 2015, p. 8.

all kinds of bad intentions, and so resentment grows and deepens. Thus, every mistake or lapse on the part of a spouse can harm the bond of love and the stability of the family. Something is wrong when we see every problem as equally serious; in this way, we risk being unduly harsh with the failings of others. The just desire to see our rights respected turns into a thirst for vengeance rather than a reasoned defence of our dignity.

106. When we have been offended or let down, forgiveness is possible and desirable, but no one can say that it is easy. The truth is that "family communion can only be preserved and perfected through a great spirit of sacrifice. It requires, in fact, a ready and generous openness of each and all to understanding, to forbearance, to pardon, to reconciliation. There is no family that does not know how selfishness, discord, tension and conflict violently attack and at times mortally wound its own communion: hence there arise the many and varied forms of division in family life".[113]

107. Today we recognize that being able to forgive others implies the liberating experience of understanding and forgiving ourselves. Often our mistakes, or criticism we have received from loved ones, can lead to a loss of self-esteem. We become distant from others, avoiding affection and fearful in our interpersonal relationships. Blaming others becomes falsely reassuring. We need to learn to pray over our past history, to accept ourselves, to learn how to live with our limitations, and even to forgive ourselves, in order to have this same attitude towards others.

108. All this assumes that we ourselves have had the experience of being forgiven by God, justified by his grace and not by our own merits. We have known a love that is prior to any of our own efforts, a love that constantly opens doors, promotes and encourages. If we accept that God's love is unconditional, that the Father's love cannot be bought or sold, then we will become capable of showing boundless love and forgiving others even if they have wronged us. Otherwise, our family life will no longer be a place of understanding, support and encouragement, but rather one of constant tension and mutual criticism.

---

[113] JOHN PAUL II, Apostolic Exhortation *Familiaris Consortio* (22 November 1981), 21: AAS 74 (1982), 106.

Love rejoices with others

109. The expression *chaírei epì te adikía* has to do with a negativity lurking deep within a person's heart. It is the toxic attitude of those who rejoice at seeing an injustice done to others. The following phrase expresses its opposite: *sygchaírei te aletheía*: "it rejoices in the right". In other words, we rejoice at the good of others when we see their dignity and value their abilities and good works. This is impossible for those who must always be comparing and competing, even with their spouse, so that they secretly rejoice in their failures.

110. When a loving person can do good for others, or sees that others are happy, they themselves live happily and in this way give glory to God, for "God loves a cheerful giver" (*2 Cor* 9:7). Our Lord especially appreciates those who find joy in the happiness of others. If we fail to learn how to rejoice in the well-being of others, and focus primarily on our own needs, we condemn ourselves to a joyless existence, for, as Jesus said, "it is more blessed to give than to receive" (*Acts* 20:35). The family must always be a place where, when something good happens to one of its members, they know that others will be there to celebrate it with them.

Love bears all things

111. Paul's list ends with four phrases containing the words "all things". Love bears all things, believes all things, hopes all things, endures all things. Here we see clearly the countercultural power of a love that is able to face whatever might threaten it.

112. First, Paul says that love "bears all things" (*panta stégei*). This is about more than simply putting up with evil; it has to do with *the use of the tongue*. The verb can mean "holding one's peace" about what may be wrong with another person. It implies limiting judgement, checking the impulse to issue a firm and ruthless condemnation: "Judge not and you will not be judged" (*Lk* 6:37). Although it runs contrary to the way we normally use our tongues, God's word tells us: "Do not speak evil against one another, brothers and sisters" (*Jas* 4:11). Being willing to speak ill of another person is a way of asserting ourselves, venting resentment and envy

without concern for the harm we may do. We often forget that slander can be quite sinful; it is a grave offence against God when it seriously harms another person's good name and causes damage that is hard to repair. Hence God's word forthrightly states that the tongue "is a world of iniquity" that "stains the whole body" (*Jas* 3:6); it is a "restless evil, full of deadly poison" (3:8). Whereas the tongue can be used to "curse those who are made in the likeness of God" (3:9), love cherishes the good name of others, even one's enemies. In seeking to uphold God's law we must never forget this specific requirement of love.

113. Married couples joined by love speak well of each other; they try to show their spouse's good side, not their weakness and faults. In any event, they keep silent rather than speak ill of them. This is not merely a way of acting in front of others; it springs from an interior attitude. Far from ingenuously claiming not to see the problems and weaknesses of others, it sees those weaknesses and faults in a wider context. It recognizes that these failings are a part of a bigger picture. We have to realize that all of us are a complex mixture of light and shadows. The other person is much more than the sum of the little things that annoy me. Love does not have to be perfect for us to value it. The other person loves me as best they can, with all their limits, but the fact that love is imperfect does not mean that it is untrue or unreal. It is real, albeit limited and earthly. If I expect too much, the other person will let me know, for he or she can neither play God nor serve all my needs. Love coexists with imperfection. It "bears all things" and can hold its peace before the limitations of the loved one.

Love believes all things

114. *Panta pisteúei.* Love believes all things. Here "belief" is not to be taken in its strict theological meaning, but more in the sense of what we mean by "trust". This goes beyond simply presuming that the other is not lying or cheating. Such basic trust recognizes God's light shining beyond the darkness, like an ember glowing beneath the ash.

115. This trust enables a relationship to be free. It means we do not have to control the other person, to follow their every step lest they escape our grip. Love trusts, it sets free, it does not try to control, possess and

dominate everything. This freedom, which fosters independence, an openness to the world around us and to new experiences, can only enrich and expand relationships. The spouses then share with one another the joy of all they have received and learned outside the family circle. At the same time, this freedom makes for sincerity and transparency, for those who know that they are trusted and appreciated can be open and hide nothing. Those who know that their spouse is always suspicious, judgmental and lacking unconditional love, will tend to keep secrets, conceal their failings and weaknesses, and pretend to be someone other than who they are. On the other hand, a family marked by loving trust, come what may, helps its members to be themselves and spontaneously to reject deceit, falsehood, and lies.

Love hopes all things

116. *Panta elpízei*. Love does not despair of the future. Following upon what has just been said, this phrase speaks of the hope of one who knows that others can change, mature and radiate unexpected beauty and untold potential. This does not mean that everything will change in this life. It does involve realizing that, though things may not always turn out as we wish, God may well make crooked lines straight and draw some good from the evil we endure in this world.

117. Here hope comes most fully into its own, for it embraces the certainty of life after death. Each person, with all his or her failings, is called to the fulness of life in heaven. There, fully transformed by Christ's resurrection, every weakness, darkness and infirmity will pass away. There the person's true being will shine forth in all its goodness and beauty. This realization helps us, amid the aggravations of this present life, to see each person from a supernatural perspective, in the light of hope, and await the fulness that he or she will receive in the heavenly kingdom, even if it is not yet visible.

Love endures all things

118. *Panta hypoménei*. This means that love bears every trial with a positive attitude. It stands firm in hostile surroundings. This "endurance"

involves not only the ability to tolerate certain aggravations, but something greater: a constant readiness to confront any challenge. It is a love that *never gives up*, even in the darkest hour. It shows a certain dogged heroism, a power to resist every negative current, an irrepressible commitment to goodness. Here I think of the words of Martin Luther King, who met every kind of trial and tribulation with fraternal love: "The person who hates you most has some good in him; even the nation that hates you most has some good in it; even the race that hates you most has some good in it. And when you come to the point that you look in the face of every man and see deep down within him what religion calls 'the image of God', you begin to love him in spite of [everything]. No matter what he does, you see God's image there. There is an element of goodness that he can never slough off... Another way that you love your enemy is this: when the opportunity presents itself for you to defeat your enemy, that is the time which you must not do it... When you rise to the level of love, of its great beauty and power, you seek only to defeat evil systems. Individuals who happen to be caught up in that system, you love, but you seek to defeat the system... Hate for hate only intensifies the existence of hate and evil in the universe. If I hit you and you hit me and I hit you back and you hit me back and so on, you see, that goes on ad infinitum. It just never ends. Somewhere somebody must have a little sense, and that's the strong person. The strong person is the person who can cut off the chain of hate, the chain of evil... Somebody must have religion enough and morality enough to cut it off and inject within the very structure of the universe that strong and powerful element of love".[114]

119. In family life, we need to cultivate that strength of love which can help us fight every evil threatening it. Love does not yield to resentment, scorn for others or the desire to hurt or to gain some advantage. The Christian ideal, especially in families, is a love that never gives up. I am sometimes amazed to see men or women who have had to separate from their spouse for their own protection, yet, because of their enduring conjugal love, still try to help them, even by enlisting others, in their moments of illness, suffering or trial. Here too we see a love that never gives up.

---

[114] MARTIN LUTHER KING JR., *Sermon delivered at Dexter Avenue Baptist Church*, Montgomery, Alabama, 17 November 1957.

GROWING IN CONJUGAL LOVE

120. Our reflection on Saint Paul's hymn to love has prepared us to discuss conjugal love. This is the love between husband and wife,[115] a love sanctified, enriched and illuminated by the grace of the sacrament of marriage. It is an "affective union",[116] spiritual and sacrificial, which combines the warmth of friendship and erotic passion, and endures long after emotions and passion subside. Pope Pius XI taught that this love permeates the duties of married life and enjoys pride of place.[117] Infused by the Holy Spirit, this powerful love is a reflection of the unbroken covenant between Christ and humanity that culminated in his self-sacrifice on the cross. "The Spirit which the Lord pours forth gives a new heart and renders man and woman capable of loving one another as Christ loved us. Conjugal love reaches that fulness to which it is interiorly ordained: conjugal charity."[118]

121. Marriage is a precious sign, for "when a man and a woman celebrate the sacrament of marriage, God is, as it were, 'mirrored' in them; he impresses in them his own features and the indelible character of his love. Marriage is the icon of God's love for us. Indeed, God is also communion: the three Persons of the Father, the Son and the Holy Spirit live eternally in perfect unity. And this is precisely the mystery of marriage: God makes of the two spouses one single existence".[119] This has concrete daily consequences, because the spouses, "in virtue of the sacrament, are invested with a true and proper mission, so that, starting with the simple ordinary things of life they can make visible the love with which Christ loves his Church and continues to give his life for her".[120]

---

[115] Thomas Aquinas calls love a *vis unitiva* (*Summa Theologiae* I, q. 20, art. 1, ad 3), echoing a phrase of Pseudo-Dionysius the Areopagite (*De Divinis Nominibus*, IV, 12: PG 3, 709).

[116] THOMAS AQUINAS, *Summa Theologiae* II-II, q. 27, art. 2.

[117] Encyclical Letter *Casti Connubii* (31 December 1930): AAS 22 (1930), 547-548.

[118] JOHN PAUL II, Apostolic Exhortation *Familiaris Consortio* (22 November 1981) 13: AAS 74 (1982), 94.

[119] *Catechesis* (2 April 2014): *L'Osservatore Romano*, 3 April 2014, p. 8.

[120] *Ibid.*

122. We should not however confuse different levels: there is no need to lay upon two limited persons the tremendous burden of having to reproduce perfectly the union existing between Christ and his Church, for marriage as a sign entails "a dynamic process..., one which advances gradually with the progressive integration of the gifts of God".[121]

Lifelong sharing

123. After the love that unites us to God, conjugal love is the "greatest form of friendship".[122] It is a union possessing all the traits of a good friendship: concern for the good of the other, reciprocity, intimacy, warmth, stability and the resemblance born of a shared life. Marriage joins to all this an indissoluble exclusivity expressed in the stable commitment to share and shape together the whole of life. Let us be honest and acknowledge the signs that this is the case. Lovers do not see their relationship as merely temporary. Those who marry do not expect their excitement to fade. Those who witness the celebration of a loving union, however fragile, trust that it will pass the test of time. Children not only want their parents to love one another, but also to be faithful and remain together. These and similar signs show that it is in the very nature of conjugal love to be definitive. The lasting union expressed by the marriage vows is more than a formality or a traditional formula; it is rooted in the natural inclinations of the human person. For believers, it is also a covenant before God that calls for fidelity: "The Lord was witness to the covenant between you and the wife of your youth, to whom you have been faithless, though she is your companion and your wife by covenant... Let none be faithless to the wife of his youth. For I hate divorce, says the Lord" (*Mal* 2:14-16).

124. A love that is weak or infirm, incapable of accepting marriage as a challenge to be taken up and fought for, reborn, renewed and reinvented until death, cannot sustain a great commitment. It will succumb to the culture of the ephemeral that prevents a constant process of growth. Yet

---

[121] JOHN PAUL II, Apostolic Exhortation *Familiaris Consortio* (22 November 1981), 9: AAS 75 (1982), 90.

[122] THOMAS AQUINAS, *Summa Contra Gentiles* III, 123; cf. ARISTOTLE, *Nicomachean Ethics*, 8, 12 (ed. Bywater, Oxford, 1984, 174).

"promising love for ever is possible when we perceive a plan bigger than our own ideas and undertakings, a plan which sustains us and enables us to surrender our future entirely to the one we love".[123] If this love is to overcome all trials and remain faithful in the face of everything, it needs the gift of grace to strengthen and elevate it. In the words of Saint Robert Bellarmine, "the fact that one man unites with one woman in an indissoluble bond, and that they remain inseparable despite every kind of difficulty, even when there is no longer hope for children, can only be the sign of a great mystery".[124]

125. Marriage is likewise a friendship marked by passion, but a passion always directed to an ever more stable and intense union. This is because "marriage was not instituted solely for the procreation of children" but also that mutual love "might be properly expressed, that it should grow and mature".[125] This unique friendship between a man and a woman acquires an all-encompassing character only within the conjugal union. Precisely as all-encompassing, this union is also exclusive, faithful and open to new life. It shares everything in constant mutual respect. The Second Vatican Council echoed this by stating that "such a love, bringing together the human and the divine, leads the partners to a free and mutual self-giving, experienced in tenderness and action, and permeating their entire lives".[126]

Joy and beauty

126. In marriage, the joy of love needs to be cultivated. When the search for pleasure becomes obsessive, it holds us in thrall and keeps us from experiencing other satisfactions. Joy, on the other hand, increases our pleasure and helps us find fulfilment in any number of things, even at those times of life when physical pleasure has ebbed. Saint Thomas Aquinas said that the word "joy" refers to an expansion of the heart.[127]

---

[123] Encyclical Letter *Lumen Fidei* (29 June 2013), 52: AAS 105 (2013), 590.

[124] *De sacramento matrimonii*, I, 2; in Id., *Disputationes*, III, 5, 3 (ed. Giuliano, Naples, 1858), 778.

[125] SECOND VATICAN ECUMENICAL COUNCIL, Pastoral Constitution on the Church in the Modern World *Gaudium et Spes*, 50.

[126] *Ibid.*, 49.

[127] Cf. *Summa Theologiae* I-II, q. 31, art. 3., ad 3.

Marital joy can be experienced even amid sorrow; it involves accepting that marriage is an inevitable mixture of enjoyment and struggles, tensions and repose, pain and relief, satisfactions and longings, annoyances and pleasures, but always on the path of friendship, which inspires married couples to care for one another: "they help and serve each other".[128]

127. The love of friendship is called "charity" when it perceives and esteems the "great worth" of another person.[129] Beauty -that "great worth" which is other than physical or psychological appeal - enables us to appreciate the sacredness of a person, without feeling the need to possess it. In a consumerist society, the sense of beauty is impoverished and so joy fades. Everything is there to be purchased, possessed or consumed, including people. Tenderness, on the other hand, is a sign of a love free of selfish possessiveness. It makes us approach a person with immense respect and a certain dread of causing them harm or taking away their freedom. Loving another person involves the joy of contemplating and appreciating their innate beauty and sacredness, which is greater than my needs. This enables me to seek their good even when they cannot belong to me, or when they are no longer physically appealing but intrusive and annoying. For "the love by which one person is pleasing to another depends on his or her giving something freely".[130]

128. The aesthetic experience of love is expressed in that "gaze" which contemplates other persons as ends in themselves, even if they are infirm, elderly or physically unattractive. A look of appreciation has enormous importance, and to begrudge it is usually hurtful. How many things do spouses and children sometimes do in order to be noticed! Much hurt and many problems result when we stop looking at one another. This lies behind the complaints and grievances we often hear in families: "My husband does not look at me; he acts as if I were invisible". "Please look at me when I am talking to you!". "My wife no longer looks at me, she only has eyes for our children". "In my own home nobody cares

---

[128] SECOND VATICAN ECUMENICAL COUNCIL, Pastoral Constitution on the Church in the Modern World *Gaudium et Spes*, 48.

[129] Cf. THOMAS AQUINAS, *Summa Theologiae* I-II, q. 26, art. 3.

[130] *Ibid.*, q. 110, art. 1.

about me; they do not even see me; it is as if I did not exist". Love opens our eyes and enables us to see, beyond all else, the great worth of a human being.

129. The joy of this contemplative love needs to be cultivated. Since we were made for love, we know that there is no greater joy than that of sharing good things: "Give, take, and treat yourself well" (*Sir* 14:16). The most intense joys in life arise when we are able to elicit joy in others, as a foretaste of heaven. We can think of the lovely scene in the film *Babette's Feast*, when the generous cook receives a grateful hug and praise: "*Ah, how you will delight the angels!*" It is a joy and a great consolation to bring delight to others, to see them enjoying themselves. This joy, the fruit of fraternal love, is not that of the vain and self-centred, but of lovers who delight in the good of those whom they love, who give freely to them and thus bear good fruit.

130. On the other hand, joy also grows through pain and sorrow. In the words of Saint Augustine, "the greater the danger in battle the greater is the joy of victory".[131] After suffering and struggling together, spouses are able to experience that it was worth it, because they achieved some good, learned something as a couple, or came to appreciate what they have. Few human joys are as deep and thrilling as those experienced by two people who love one another and have achieved something as the result of a great, shared effort.

Marrying for love

131. I would like to say to young people that none of this is jeopardized when their love finds expression in marriage. Their union encounters in this institution the means to ensure that their love truly will endure and grow. Naturally, love is much more than an outward consent or a contract, yet it is nonetheless true that choosing to give marriage a visible form in society by undertaking certain commitments shows how important it is. It manifests the seriousness of each person's identification with the other and their firm decision to leave adolescent individualism behind and to belong

---

[131] AUGUSTINE, *Confessions*, VIII, III, 7: PL 32, 752.

to one another. Marriage is a means of expressing that we have truly left the security of the home in which we grew up in order to build other strong ties and to take on a new responsibility for another person. This is much more meaningful than a mere spontaneous association for mutual gratification, which would turn marriage into a purely private affair. As a social institution, marriage protects and shapes a shared commitment to deeper growth in love and commitment to one another, for the good of society as a whole. That is why marriage is more than a fleeting fashion; it is of enduring importance. Its essence derives from our human nature and social character. It involves a series of obligations born of love itself, a love so serious and generous that it is ready to face any risk.

132. To opt for marriage in this way expresses a genuine and firm decision to join paths, come what may. Given its seriousness, this public commitment of love cannot be the fruit of a hasty decision, but neither can it be postponed indefinitely. Committing oneself exclusively and definitively to another person always involves a risk and a bold gamble. Unwillingness to make such a commitment is selfish, calculating and petty. It fails to recognize the rights of another person and to present him or her to society as someone worthy of unconditional love. If two persons are truly in love, they naturally show this to others. When love is expressed before others in the marriage contract, with all its public commitments, it clearly indicates and protects the "yes" which those persons speak freely and unreservedly to each other. This "yes" tells them that they can always trust one another, and that they will never be abandoned when difficulties arise or new attractions or selfish interests present themselves.

A love that reveals itself and increases

133. The love of friendship unifies all aspects of marital life and helps family members to grow constantly. This love must be freely and generously expressed in words and acts. In the family, "three words need to be used. I want to repeat this! Three words: 'Please', 'Thank you', 'Sorry'. Three essential words!"[132] "In our families when we are not

---

[132] *Address to the Pilgrimage of Families during the Year of Faith* (26 October 2013): AAS 105 (2013), 980.

overbearing and ask: 'May I?'; in our families when we are not selfish and can say: 'Thank you!'; and in our families when someone realizes that he or she did something wrong and is able to say 'Sorry!', our family experiences peace and joy".[133] Let us not be stingy about using these words, but keep repeating them, day after day. For "certain silences are oppressive, even at times within families, between husbands and wives, between parents and children, among siblings".[134] The right words, spoken at the right time, daily protect and nurture love.

134. All this occurs through a process of constant growth. The very special form of love that is marriage is called to embody what Saint Thomas Aquinas said about charity in general. "Charity", he says, "by its very nature, has no limit to its increase, for it is a participation in that infinite charity which is the Holy Spirit... Nor on the part of the subject can its limit be fixed, because as charity grows, so too does its capacity for an even greater increase".[135] Saint Paul also prays: "May the Lord make you increase and abound in love to one another" (*1 Th* 3:12), and again, "concerning fraternal love... we urge you, beloved, to do so more and more" (*1 Th* 4:9-10). More and more! Marital love is not defended primarily by presenting indissolubility as a duty, or by repeating doctrine, but by helping it to grow ever stronger under the impulse of grace. A love that fails to grow is at risk. Growth can only occur if we respond to God's grace through constant acts of love, acts of kindness that become ever more frequent, intense, generous, tender and cheerful. Husbands and wives "become conscious of their unity and experience it more deeply from day to day".[136] The gift of God's love poured out upon the spouses is also a summons to constant growth in grace.

135. It is not helpful to dream of an idyllic and perfect love needing no stimulus to grow. A celestial notion of earthly love forgets that the best

---

[133] *Angelus Message* (29 December 2013): *L'Osservatore Romano*, 30-31 December 2013, p. 7.

[134] *Address to the Pilgrimage of Families during the Year of Faith* (26 October 2013): AAS 105 (2013), 978.

[135] *Summa Theologiae* II-II, q. 24, art. 7.

[136] SECOND VATICAN ECUMENICAL COUNCIL, Pastoral Constitution on the Church in the Modern World *Gaudium et Spes*, 48.

is yet to come, that fine wine matures with age. As the Bishops of Chile have pointed out, "the perfect families proposed by deceptive consumerist propaganda do not exist. In those families, no one grows old, there is no sickness, sorrow or death... Consumerist propaganda presents a fantasy that has nothing to do with the reality which must daily be faced by the heads of families".[137] It is much healthier to be realistic about our limits, defects and imperfections, and to respond to the call to grow together, to bring love to maturity and to strengthen the union, come what may.

Dialogue

136. Dialogue is essential for experiencing, expressing and fostering love in marriage and family life. Yet it can only be the fruit of a long and demanding apprenticeship. Men and women, young people and adults, communicate differently. They speak different languages and they act in different ways. Our way of asking and responding to questions, the tone we use, our timing and any number of other factors condition how well we communicate. We need to develop certain attitudes that express love and encourage authentic dialogue.

137. Take time, quality time. This means being ready to listen patiently and attentively to everything the other person wants to say. It requires the self-discipline of not speaking until the time is right. Instead of offering an opinion or advice, we need to be sure that we have heard everything the other person has to say. This means cultivating an interior silence that makes it possible to listen to the other person without mental or emotional distractions. Do not be rushed, put aside all of your own needs and worries, and make space. Often the other spouse does not need a solution to his or her problems, but simply to be heard, to feel that someone has acknowledge their pain, their disappointment, their fear, their anger, their hopes and their dreams. How often we hear complaints like: "He does not listen to me." "Even when you seem to, you are really doing something else." "I talk to her and I feel like she can't wait for me to finish." "When I speak to her, she tries to change the subject, or she gives me curt responses to end the conversation".

---

[137] CHILEAN BISHOPS' CONFERENCE, *La vida y la familia: regalos de Dios para cada uno de nosotros* (21 July 2014).

138. Develop the habit of giving real importance to the other person. This means appreciating them and recognizing their right to exist, to think as they do and to be happy. Never downplay what they say or think, even if you need to express your own point of view. Everyone has something to contribute, because they have their life experiences, they look at things from a different standpoint and they have their own concerns, abilities and insights. We ought to be able to acknowledge the other person's truth, the value of his or her deepest concerns, and what it is that they are trying to communicate, however aggressively. We have to put ourselves in their shoes and try to peer into their hearts, to perceive their deepest concerns and to take them as a point of departure for further dialogue.

139. Keep an open mind. Don't get bogged down in your own limited ideas and opinions, but be prepared to change or expand them. The combination of two different ways of thinking can lead to a synthesis that enriches both. The unity that we seek is not uniformity, but a "unity in diversity", or "reconciled diversity". Fraternal communion is enriched by respect and appreciation for differences within an overall perspective that advances the common good. We need to free ourselves from feeling that we all have to be alike. A certain astuteness is also needed to prevent the appearance of "static" that can interfere with the process of dialogue. For example, if hard feelings start to emerge, they should be dealt with sensitively, lest they interrupt the dynamic of dialogue. The ability to say what one is thinking without offending the other person is important. Words should be carefully chosen so as not to offend, especially when discussing difficult issues. Making a point should never involve venting anger and inflicting hurt. A patronizing tone only serves to hurt, ridicule, accuse and offend others. Many disagreements between couples are not about important things. Mostly they are about trivial matters. What alters the mood, however, is the way things are said or the attitude with which they are said.

140. Show affection and concern for the other person. Love surmounts even the worst barriers. When we love someone, or when we feel loved by them, we can better understand what they are trying to communicate. Fearing the other person as a kind of "rival" is a sign of weakness and

needs to be overcome. It is very important to base one's position on solid choices, beliefs or values, and not on the need to win an argument or to be proved right.

141. Finally, let us acknowledge that for a worthwhile dialogue we have to have something to say. This can only be the fruit of an interior richness nourished by reading, personal reflection, prayer and openness to the world around us. Otherwise, conversations become boring and trivial. When neither of the spouses works at this, and has little real contact with other people, family life becomes stifling and dialogue impoverished.

PASSIONATE LOVE

142. The Second Vatican Council teaches that this conjugal love "embraces the good of the whole person; it can enrich the sentiments of the spirit and their physical expression with a unique dignity and ennoble them as the special features and manifestation of the friendship proper to marriage".[138] For this reason, a love lacking either pleasure or passion is insufficient to symbolize the union of the human heart with God: "All the mystics have affirmed that supernatural love and heavenly love find the symbols which they seek in marital love, rather than in friendship, filial devotion or devotion to a cause. And the reason is to be found precisely in its totality".[139] Why then should we not pause to speak of feelings and sexuality in marriage?

The world of emotions

143. Desires, feelings, emotions, what the ancients called "the passions", all have an important place in married life. They are awakened whenever "another" becomes present and part of a person's life. It is characteristic of all living beings to reach out to other things, and this tendency always has basic affective signs: pleasure or pain, joy or sadness, tenderness or fear. They ground the most elementary psychological activity. Human beings live on this earth, and all that they do and seek is fraught with passion.

---

[138] Pastoral Constitution on the Church in the Modern World *Gaudium et Spes*, 49.

[139] A. SERTILLANGES, *L'Amour chrétien*, Paris, 1920, 174.

144. As true man, Jesus showed his emotions. He was hurt by the rejection of Jerusalem (cf. *Mt* 23:27) and this moved him to tears (cf. *Lk* 19:41). He was also deeply moved by the sufferings of others (cf. *Mk* 6:34). He felt deeply their grief (cf. *Jn* 11:33), and he wept at the death of a friend (cf. *Jn* 11:35). These examples of his sensitivity showed how much his human heart was open to others.

145. Experiencing an emotion is not, in itself, morally good or evil.[140] The stirring of desire or repugnance is neither sinful nor blameworthy. What is morally good or evil is what we do on the basis of, or under the influence of, a given passion. But when passions are aroused or sought, and as a result we perform evil acts, the evil lies in the decision to fuel them and in the evil acts that result. Along the same lines, my being attracted to someone is not automatically good. If my attraction to that person makes me try to dominate him or her, then my feeling only serves my selfishness. To believe that we are good simply because "we feel good" is a tremendous illusion. There are those who feel themselves capable of great love only because they have a great need for affection, yet they prove incapable of the effort needed to bring happiness to others. They remain caught up in their own needs and desires. In such cases, emotions distract from the highest values and conceal a self-centredness that makes it impossible to develop a healthy and happy family life.

146. This being said, if passion accompanies a free act, it can manifest the depth of that act. Marital love strives to ensure that one's entire emotional life benefits the family as a whole and stands at the service of its common life. A family is mature when the emotional life of its members becomes a form of sensitivity that neither stifles nor obscures great decisions and values, but rather follows each one's freedom,[141] springs from it, enriches, perfects and harmonizes it in the service of all.

God loves the joy of his children

147. This calls for a pedagogical process that involves renunciation. This conviction on the part of the Church has often been rejected as

---

[140] Cf. THOMAS AQUINAS, *Summa Theologiae* I-II, q. 24, art. 1.

[141] Cf. *ibid.*, q. 59, art. 5.

opposed to human happiness. Benedict XVI summed up this charge with great clarity: "Doesn't the Church, with all her commandments and prohibitions, turn to bitterness the most precious thing in life? Doesn't she blow the whistle just when the joy which is the Creator's gift offers us a happiness which is itself a certain foretaste of the Divine?"[142] He responded that, although there have been exaggerations and deviant forms of asceticism in Christianity, the Church's official teaching, in fidelity to the Scriptures, did not reject "*eros* as such, but rather declared war on a warped and destructive form of it, because this counterfeit divinization of *eros*... actually strips it of divine dignity and dehumanizes it".[143]

148. Training in the areas of emotion and instinct is necessary, and at times this requires setting limits. Excess, lack of control or obsession with a single form of pleasure can end up weakening and tainting that very pleasure[144] and damaging family life. A person can certainly channel his passions in a beautiful and healthy way, increasingly pointing them towards altruism and an integrated self-fulfilment that can only enrich interpersonal relationships in the heart of the family. This does not mean renouncing moments of intense enjoyment,[145] but rather integrating them with other moments of generous commitment, patient hope, inevitable weariness and struggle to achieve an ideal. Family life is all this, and it deserves to be lived to the fullest.

149. Some currents of spirituality teach that desire has to be eliminated as a path to liberation from pain. Yet we believe that God loves the enjoyment felt by human beings: he created us and "richly furnishes us with everything to enjoy" (*1 Tim* 6:17). Let us be glad when with great love he tells us: "My son, treat yourself well... Do not deprive yourself of a happy day" (*Sir* 14:11-14). Married couples likewise respond to God's will when they take up the biblical injunction: "Be joyful in the

---

[142] Encyclical Letter *Deus Caritas Est* (25 December 2005), 3: AAS 98 (2006), 219-220.

[143] *Ibid.*, 4: AAS 98 (2006), 220.

[144] Cf. THOMAS AQUINAS, *Summa Theologiae* I-II, q. 32, art.7.

[145] Cf. id., *Summa Theologiae* II-II, q. 153, art. 2, ad 2: *"Abundantia delectationis quae est in actu venereo secundum rationem ordinato, non contrariatur medio virtutis"*.

day of prosperity" (*Ec* 7:14). What is important is to have the freedom to realize that pleasure can find different expressions at different times of life, in accordance with the needs of mutual love. In this sense, we can appreciate the teachings of some Eastern masters who urge us to expand our consciousness, lest we be imprisoned by one limited experience that can blinker us. This expansion of consciousness is not the denial or destruction of desire so much as its broadening and perfection.

The erotic dimension of love

150. All this brings us to the sexual dimension of marriage. God himself created sexuality, which is a marvellous gift to his creatures. If this gift needs to be cultivated and directed, it is to prevent the "impoverishment of an authentic value".[146] Saint John Paul II rejected the claim that the Church's teaching is "a negation of the value of human sexuality", or that the Church simply tolerates sexuality "because it is necessary for procreation".[147] Sexual desire is not something to be looked down upon, and "and there can be no attempt whatsoever to call into question its necessity".[148]

151. To those who fear that the training of the passions and of sexuality detracts from the spontaneity of sexual love, Saint John Paul II replied that human persons are "called to full and mature spontaneity in their relationships", a maturity that "is the gradual fruit of a discernment of the impulses of one's own heart".[149] This calls for discipline and self-mastery, since every human person "must learn, with perseverance and consistency, the meaning of his or her body".[150] Sexuality is not a means of gratification or entertainment; it is an interpersonal language wherein the other is taken seriously, in his or her sacred and inviolable dignity. As such, "the human heart comes to participate, so to speak, in another kind of spontaneity".[151] In this context, the erotic appears

---

[146] JOHN PAUL II, *Catechesis* (22 October 1980), 5: *Insegnamenti* III/2 (1980), 951.

[147] *Ibid.*, 3.

[148] ID., *Catechesis*, (24 September 1980), 4: *Insegnamenti* III/2 (1980), 719.

[149] *Catechesis* (12 November 1980), 2: *Insegnamenti* III/2 (1980), 1133.

[150] *Ibid.*, 4.

[151] *Ibid.*, 5.

as a specifically human manifestation of sexuality. It enables us to discover "the nuptial meaning of the body and the authentic dignity of the gift".[152] In his catecheses on the theology of the body, Saint John Paul II taught that sexual differentiation not only is "a source of fruitfulness and procreation", but also possesses "the capacity of expressing love: that love precisely in which the human person becomes a gift".[153] A healthy sexual desire, albeit closely joined to a pursuit of pleasure, always involves a sense of wonder, and for that very reason can humanize the impulses.

152. In no way, then, can we consider the erotic dimension of love simply as a permissible evil or a burden to be tolerated for the good of the family. Rather, it must be seen as gift from God that enriches the relationship of the spouses. As a passion sublimated by a love respectful of the dignity of the other, it becomes a "pure, unadulterated affirmation" revealing the marvels of which the human heart is capable. In this way, even momentarily, we can feel that "life has turned out good and happy".[154]

Violence and manipulation

153. On the basis of this positive vision of sexuality, we can approach the entire subject with a healthy realism. It is, after all, a fact that sex often becomes depersonalized and unhealthy; as a result, "it becomes the occasion and instrument for self-assertion and the selfish satisfaction of personal desires and instincts".[155] In our own day, sexuality risks being poisoned by the mentality of "use and discard". The body of the other is often viewed as an object to be used as long as it offers satisfaction, and rejected once it is no longer appealing. Can we really ignore or overlook the continuing forms of domination, arrogance, abuse, sexual perversion and violence that are the product

---

[152] *Ibid.*, 1: 1132.

[153] *Catechesis* (16 January 1980), 1: *Insegnamenti* III/1 (1980), 151.

[154] JOSEF PIEPER, *Über die Liebe*, Munich, 2014, 174. English: *On Love*, in *Faith, Hope, Love*, San Francisco, 1997, p. 256.

[155] JOHN PAUL II, Encyclical Letter *Evangelium Vitae* (25 March 1995), 23: AAS 87 (1995), 427.

of a warped understanding of sexuality? Or the fact that the dignity of others and our human vocation to love thus end up being less important than an obscure need to "find oneself"?

154. We also know that, within marriage itself, sex can become a source of suffering and manipulation. Hence it must be clearly reaffirmed that "a conjugal act imposed on one's spouse without regard to his or her condition, or personal and reasonable wishes in the matter, is no true act of love, and therefore offends the moral order in its particular application to the intimate relationship of husband and wife".[156] The acts proper to the sexual union of husband and wife correspond to the nature of sexuality as willed by God when they take place in "a manner which is truly human".[157] Saint Paul insists: "Let no one transgress and wrong his brother or sister in this matter" (*1 Th* 4:6). Even though Paul was writing in the context of a patriarchal culture in which women were considered completely subordinate to men, he nonetheless taught that sex must involve communication between the spouses: he brings up the possibility of postponing sexual relations for a period, but "by agreement" (*1 Cor* 7:5).

155. Saint John Paul II very subtly warned that a couple can be "threatened by insatiability"[158]. In other words, while called to an increasingly profound union, they can risk effacing their differences and the rightful distance between the two. For each possesses his or her own proper and inalienable dignity. When reciprocal belonging turns into domination, "the structure of communion in interpersonal relations is essentially changed".[159] It is part of the mentality of domination that those who dominate end up negating their own dignity.[160] Ultimately, they no longer "identify themselves subjectively with their own body",[161] because

---

[156] Paul VI, Encyclical Letter *Humanae Vitae* (25 July 1968), 13: AAS 60 (1968), 489.

[157] Second Vatican Ecumenical Council, Pastoral Constitution on the Church in the Modern World *Gaudium et Spes*, 49.

[158] *Catechesis* (18 June 1980), 5: *Insegnamenti* III/1 (1980), 1778.

[159] *Ibid.*, 6.

[160] Cf. *Catechesis* (30 July 1980), 1: *Insegnamenti* III/2 (1980), 311.

[161] *Catechesis* (8 April 1981), 3: *Insegnamenti* IV/1 (1981), 904.

they take away its deepest meaning. They end up using sex as form of escapism and renounce the beauty of conjugal union.

156. Every form of sexual submission must be clearly rejected. This includes all improper interpretations of the passage in the Letter to the Ephesians where Paul tells women to "be subject to your husbands" (*Eph* 5:22). This passage mirrors the cultural categories of the time, but our concern is not with its cultural matrix but with the revealed message that it conveys. As Saint John Paul II wisely observed: "Love excludes every kind of subjection whereby the wife might become a servant or a slave of the husband... The community or unity which they should establish through marriage is constituted by a reciprocal donation of self, which is also a mutual subjection".[162] Hence Paul goes on to say that "husbands should love their wives as their own bodies" (*Eph* 5:28). The biblical text is actually concerned with encouraging everyone to overcome a complacent individualism and to be constantly mindful of others: "Be subject to one another" (*Eph* 5:21). In marriage, this reciprocal "submission" takes on a special meaning, and is seen as a freely chosen mutual belonging marked by fidelity, respect and care. Sexuality is inseparably at the service of this conjugal friendship, for it is meant to aid the fulfilment of the other.

157. All the same, the rejection of distortions of sexuality and eroticism should never lead us to a disparagement or neglect of sexuality and *eros* in themselves. The ideal of marriage cannot be seen purely as generous donation and self-sacrifice, where each spouse renounces all personal needs and seeks only the other's good without concern for personal satisfaction. We need to remember that authentic love also needs to be able to receive the other, to accept one's own vulnerability and needs, and to welcome with sincere and joyful gratitude the physical expressions of love found in a caress, an embrace, a kiss and sexual union. Benedict XVI stated this very clearly: "Should man aspire to be pure spirit and to reject the flesh as pertaining to his animal nature alone, then spirit and body would both lose their dignity".[163] For this reason, "man cannot live by oblative, descending love alone. He cannot always give, he must also

---

[162] *Catechesis* (11 August 1982), 4: *Insegnamenti* V/3 (1982), 205-206.

[163] Encyclical Letter *Deus Caritas Est* (25 December 2005), 5: AAS 98 (2006), 221.

receive. Anyone who wishes to give love must also receive love as a gift".[164] Still, we must never forget that our human equilibrium is fragile; there is a part of us that resists real human growth, and any moment it can unleash the most primitive and selfish tendencies.

Marriage and virginity

158. "Many people who are unmarried are not only devoted to their own family but often render great service in their group of friends, in the Church community and in their professional lives. Sometimes their presence and contributions are overlooked, causing in them a sense of isolation. Many put their talents at the service of the Christian community through charity and volunteer work. Others remain unmarried because they consecrate their lives to the love of Christ and neighbour. Their dedication greatly enriches the family, the Church and society".[165]

159. Virginity is a form of love. As a sign, it speaks to us of the coming of the Kingdom and the need for complete devotion to the cause of the Gospel (cf. *1 Cor* 7:32). It is also a reflection of the fulness of heaven, where "they neither marry not are given in marriage" (*Mt* 22:30). Saint Paul recommended virginity because he expected Jesus' imminent return and he wanted everyone to concentrate only on spreading the Gospel: "the appointed time has grown very short" (*1 Cor* 7:29). Nonetheless, he made it clear that this was his personal opinion and preference (cf. *1 Cor* 7:6-9), not something demanded by Christ: "I have no command in the Lord" (*1 Cor* 7:25). All the same, he recognized the value of the different callings: "Each has his or her own special gift from God, one of one kind and one of another" (*1 Cor* 7:7). Reflecting on this, Saint John Paul II noted that the biblical texts "give no reason to assert the 'inferiority' of marriage, nor the 'superiority' of virginity or celibacy"[166] based on sexual abstinence. Rather than speak absolutely of the superiority of virginity, it should be enough to point out that the different states of life complement one another, and consequently that some can be more perfect in one way

---

[164] *Ibid.*, 7.

[165] *Relatio Finalis* 2015, 22.

[166] *Catechesis* (14 April 1982), 1: *Insegnamenti* V/1 (1982), 1176.

and others in another. Alexander of Hales, for example, stated that in one sense marriage may be considered superior to the other sacraments, inasmuch as it symbolizes the great reality of "Christ's union with the Church, or the union of his divine and human natures".[167]

160. Consequently, "it is not a matter of diminishing the value of matrimony in favour of continence".[168] "There is no basis for playing one off against the other... If, following a certain theological tradition, one speaks of a 'state of perfection' (*status perfectionis*), this has to do not with continence in itself, but with the entirety of a life based on the evangelical counsels".[169] A married person can experience the highest degree of charity and thus "reach the perfection which flows from charity, through fidelity to the spirit of those counsels. Such perfection is possible and accessible to every man and woman".[170]

161. The value of virginity lies in its symbolizing a love that has no need to possess the other; in this way it reflects the freedom of the Kingdom of Heaven. Virginity encourages married couples to live their own conjugal love against the backdrop of Christ's definitive love, journeying together towards the fulness of the Kingdom. For its part, conjugal love symbolizes other values. On the one hand, it is a particular reflection of that full unity in distinction found in the Trinity. The family is also a sign of Christ. It manifests the closeness of God who is a part of every human life, since he became one with us through his incarnation, death and resurrection. Each spouse becomes "one flesh" with the other as a sign of willingness to share everything with him or her until death. Whereas virginity is an "eschatological" sign of the risen Christ, marriage is a "historical" sign for us living in this world, a sign of the earthly Christ who chose to become one with us and gave himself up for us even to shedding his blood. Virginity and marriage are, and must be, different ways of loving. For "man

---

[167] *Glossa in quatuor libros sententiarum Petri Lombardi*, IV, XXVI, 2 (Quaracchi, 1957, 446).

[168] JOHN PAUL II, *Catechesis* (7 April 1982), 2: *Insegnamenti* V/1 (1982), 1127.

[169] Id., *Catechesis* (14 April 1982), 3: *Insegnamenti* V/1 (1982), 1177.

[170] *Ibid.*

cannot live without love. He remains a being that is incomprehensible for himself, his life is senseless, if love is not revealed to him".[171]

162. Celibacy can risk becoming a comfortable single life that provides the freedom to be independent, to move from one residence, work or option to another, to spend money as one sees fit and to spend time with others as one wants. In such cases, the witness of married people becomes especially eloquent. Those called to virginity can encounter in some marriages a clear sign of God's generous and steadfast fidelity to his covenant, and this can move them to a more concrete and generous availability to others. Many married couples remain faithful when one of them has become physically unattractive, or fails to satisfy the other's needs, despite the voices in our society that might encourage them to be unfaithful or to leave the other. A wife can care for her sick husband and thus, in drawing near to the Cross, renew her commitment to love unto death. In such love, the dignity of the true lover shines forth, inasmuch as it is more proper to charity to love than to be loved.[172] We could also point to the presence in many families of a capacity for selfless and loving service when children prove troublesome and even ungrateful. This makes those parents a sign of the free and selfless love of Jesus. Cases like these encourage celibate persons to live their commitment to the Kingdom with greater generosity and openness. Today, secularization has obscured the value of a life-long union and the beauty of the vocation to marriage. For this reason, it is "necessary to deepen an understanding of the *positive* aspects of conjugal love".[173]

THE TRANSFORMATION OF LOVE

163. Longer life spans now mean that close and exclusive relationships must last for four, five or even six decades; consequently, the initial decision has to be frequently renewed. While one of the spouses may no longer experience an intense sexual desire for the other, he or she may still experience the pleasure of mutual belonging and the knowledge that neither of them is alone but has a "partner" with whom everything in life

---

[171] ID., Encyclical Letter *Redemptor Hominis* (4 March 1979), 10: AAS 71 (1979), 274.

[172] Cf. Thomas Aquinas, *Summa Theologiae*, II-II, q. 27, art. 1.

[173] Pontifical Council for the Family, *Family, Marriage and "De Facto" Unions* (26 July 2000), 40.

is shared. He or she is a companion on life's journey, one with whom to face life's difficulties and enjoy its pleasures. This satisfaction is part of the affection proper to conjugal love. There is no guarantee that we will feel the same way all through life. Yet if a couple can come up with a shared and lasting life project, they can love one another and live as one until death do them part, enjoying an enriching intimacy. The love they pledge is greater than any emotion, feeling or state of mind, although it may include all of these. It is a deeper love, a lifelong decision of the heart. Even amid unresolved conflicts and confused emotional situations, they daily reaffirm their decision to love, to belong to one another, to share their lives and to continue loving and forgiving. Each progresses along the path of personal growth and development. On this journey, love rejoices at every step and in every new stage.

164. In the course of every marriage physical appearances change, but this hardly means that love and attraction need fade. We love the other person for who they are, not simply for their body. Although the body ages, it still expresses that personal identity that first won our heart. Even if others can no longer see the beauty of that identity, a spouse continues to see it with the eyes of love and so his or her affection does not diminish. He or she reaffirms the decision to belong to the other and expresses that choice in faithful and loving closeness. The nobility of this decision, by its intensity and depth, gives rise to a new kind of emotion as they fulfil their marital mission. For "emotion, caused by another human being as a person... does not *per se* tend toward the conjugal act".[174] It finds other sensible expressions. Indeed, love "is a single reality, but with different dimensions; at different times, one or other dimension may emerge more clearly".[175] The marriage bond finds new forms of expression and constantly seeks new ways to grow in strength. These both preserve and strengthen the bond. They call for daily effort. None of this, however, is possible without praying to the Holy Spirit for an outpouring of his grace, his supernatural strength and his spiritual fire, to confirm, direct and transform our love in every new situation.

---

[174] JOHN PAUL II, *Catechesis* (31 October 1984), 6: *Insegnamenti* VII/2 (1984), 1072.

[175] BENEDICT XVI, Encyclical Letter *Deus Caritas Est* (25 December 2005), 8: AAS 98 (2006), 224.

CHAPTER FIVE

LOVE MADE FRUITFUL

165. Love always gives life. Conjugal love "does not end with the couple... The couple, in giving themselves to one another, give not just themselves but also the reality of children, who are a living reflection of their love, a permanent sign of their conjugal unity and a living and inseparable synthesis of their being a father and a mother".[176]

WELCOMING A NEW LIFE

166. The family is the setting in which a new life is not only born but also welcomed as a gift of God. Each new life "allows us to appreciate the utterly gratuitous dimension of love, which never ceases to amaze us. It is the beauty of being loved first: children are loved even before they arrive".[177] Here we see a reflection of the primacy of the love of God, who always takes the initiative, for children "are loved before having done anything to deserve it".[178] And yet, "from the first moments of their lives, many children are rejected, abandoned, and robbed of their childhood and future. There are those who dare to say, as if to justify themselves, that it was a mistake to bring these children into the world. This is shameful! ... How can we issue solemn declarations on human rights and the rights of children, if we then punish children for the errors of adults?"[179] If a child comes into this world in unwanted circumstances, the parents and other members of the family must do everything possible to accept that child as a gift from God and assume the responsibility of accepting him or her with openness and affection. For "when speaking of children who come into the world, no sacrifice made by adults will be considered too costly or too great, if it means the child never has to feel that he or she is a mistake, or worthless or

---

[176] John Paul II, Apostolic Exhortation *Familiaris Consortio*, (22 November 1981), 14: AAS 74 (1982), 96.

[177] *Catechesis* (11 February 2015): *L'Osservatore Romano*, 12 February 2015, p. 8.

[178] *Ibid.*

[179] *Catechesis* (8 April 2015): *L'Osservatore Romano*, 9 April 2015, p. 8.

abandoned to the four winds and the arrogance of man".[180] The gift of a new child, entrusted by the Lord to a father and a mother, begins with acceptance, continues with lifelong protection and has as its final goal the joy of eternal life. By serenely contemplating the ultimate fulfilment of each human person, parents will be even more aware of the precious gift entrusted to them. For God allows parents to choose the name by which he himself will call their child for all eternity.[181]

167. Large families are a joy for the Church. They are an expression of the fruitfulness of love. At the same time, Saint John Paul II rightly explained that responsible parenthood does not mean "unlimited procreation or lack of awareness of what is involved in rearing children, but rather the empowerment of couples to use their inviolable liberty wisely and responsibly, taking into account social and demographic realities, as well as their own situation and legitimate desires".[182]

Love and pregnancy

168. Pregnancy is a difficult but wonderful time. A mother joins with God to bring forth the miracle of a new life. Motherhood is the fruit of a "particular creative potential of the female body, directed to the conception and birth of a new human being".[183] Each woman shares in "the mystery of creation, which is renewed with each birth".[184] The Psalmist says: "You knit me together in my mother's womb" (*Ps* 139:13). Every child growing within the mother's womb is part of the eternal loving plan of God the Father: "Before I formed you in the womb I knew you, and before you were born I consecrated you" (*Jer* 1:5). Each child has a place in God's heart from all eternity; once he or she is conceived, the Creator's eternal dream comes true. Let us pause to think of the great value of that embryo

---

[180] *Ibid.*

[181] Cf. SECOND VATICAN ECUMENICAL COUNCIL, Pastoral Constitution on the Church in the Modern World *Gaudium et Spes*, 51: "Let us all be convinced that human life and its transmission are realities whose meaning is not limited by the horizons of this life only: their true evaluation and full meaning can only be understood in reference to our eternal destiny".

[182] *Letter to the Secretary General of the United Nations Organization on Population and Development* (18 March 1994): *Insegnamenti* XVII/1 (1994), 750-751.

[183] JOHN PAUL II, *Catechesis* (12 March 1980), 3: *Insegnamenti* III/1 (1980), 543.

[184] *Ibid.*

from the moment of conception. We need to see it with the eyes of God, who always looks beyond mere appearances.

169. A pregnant woman can participate in God's plan by dreaming of her child. "For nine months every mother and father dreams about their child... You can't have a family without dreams. Once a family loses the ability to dream, children do not grow, love does not grow, life shrivels up and dies".[185] For Christian married couples, baptism necessarily appears as a part of that dream. With their prayers, parents prepare for baptism, entrusting their baby to Jesus even before he or she is born.

170. Scientific advances today allow us to know beforehand what colour a child's hair will be or what illnesses they may one day suffer, because all the somatic traits of the person are written in his or her genetic code already in the embryonic stage. Yet only the Father, the Creator, fully knows the child; he alone knows his or her deepest identity and worth. Expectant mothers need to ask God for the wisdom fully to know their children and to accept them as they are. Some parents feel that their child is not coming at the best time. They should ask the Lord to heal and strengthen them to accept their child fully and wholeheartedly. It is important for that child to feel wanted. He or she is not an accessory or a solution to some personal need. A child is a human being of immense worth and may never be used for one's own benefit. So it matters little whether this new life is convenient for you, whether it has features that please you, or whether it fits into your plans and aspirations. For "children are a gift. Each one is unique and irreplaceable... We love our children because they are children, not because they are beautiful, or look or think as we do, or embody our dreams. We love them because they are children. A child is a child".[186] The love of parents is the means by which God our Father shows his own love. He awaits the birth of each child, accepts that child unconditionally, and welcomes him or her freely.

---

[185] *Address at the Meeting with Families in Manila* (16 January 2015): AAS 107 (2015), 176.

[186] *Catechesis* (11 February 2015): *L'Osservatore Romano*, 12 February 2015, p. 8.

171. With great affection I urge all future mothers: keep happy and let nothing rob you of the interior joy of motherhood. Your child deserves your happiness. Don't let fears, worries, other people's comments or problems lessen your joy at being God's means of bringing a new life to the world. Prepare yourself for the birth of your child, but without obsessing, and join in Mary's song of joy: "My soul proclaims the greatness of the Lord and my spirit exults in God my Saviour, for he has looked with favour on the lowliness of his servant" (*Lk* 1:46-48). Try to experience this serene excitement amid all your many concerns, and ask the Lord to preserve your joy, so that you can pass it on to your child.

The love of a mother and a father

172. "Children, once born, begin to receive, along with nourishment and care, the spiritual gift of knowing with certainty that they are loved. This love is shown to them through the gift of their personal name, the sharing of language, looks of love and the brightness of a smile. In this way, they learn that the beauty of human relationships touches our soul, seeks our freedom, accepts the difference of others, recognizes and respects them as a partner in dialogue... Such is love, and it contains a spark of God's love!"[187] Every child has a right to receive love from a mother and a father; both are necessary for a child's integral and harmonious development. As the Australian Bishops have observed, each of the spouses "contributes in a distinct way to the upbringing of a child. Respecting a child's dignity means affirming his or her need and natural right to have a mother and a father".[188] We are speaking not simply of the love of father and mother as individuals, but also of their mutual love, perceived as the source of one's life and the solid foundation of the family. Without this, a child could become a mere plaything. Husband and wife, father and mother, both "co-operate with the love of God the Creator, and are, in a certain sense, his interpreters".[189] They show their children the maternal and paternal face of the Lord. Together they teach the value of reciprocity, of respect

---

[187] *Catechesis* (14 October 2015): *L'Osservatore Romano*, 15 October 2015, p. 8.

[188] AUSTRALIAN CATHOLIC BISHOPS' CONFERENCE, Pastoral Letter *Don't Mess with Marriage* (24 November 2015), 13.

[189] SECOND VATICAN ECUMENICAL COUNCIL, Pastoral Constitution on the Church in the Modern World *Gaudium et Spes*, 50.

for differences and of being able to give and take. If for some inevitable reason one parent should be lacking, it is important to compensate for this loss, for the sake of the child's healthy growth to maturity.

173. The sense of being orphaned that affects many children and young people today is much deeper than we think. Nowadays we acknowledge as legitimate and indeed desirable that women wish to study, work, develop their skills and have personal goals. At the same time, we cannot ignore the need that children have for a mother's presence, especially in the first months of life. Indeed, "the woman stands before the man as a mother, the subject of the new human life that is conceived and develops in her, and from her is born into the world".[190] The weakening of this maternal presence with its feminine qualities poses a grave risk to our world. I certainly value feminism, but one that does not demand uniformity or negate motherhood. For the grandeur of women includes all the rights derived from their inalienable human dignity but also from their feminine genius, which is essential to society. Their specifically feminine abilities - motherhood in particular - also grant duties, because womanhood also entails a specific mission in this world, a mission that society needs to protect and preserve for the good of all.[191]

174. "Mothers are the strongest antidote to the spread of self-centred individualism... It is they who testify to the beauty of life".[192] Certainly, "a society without mothers would be dehumanized, for mothers are always, even in the worst of times, witnesses to tenderness, dedication and moral strength. Mothers often communicate the deepest meaning of religious practice in the first prayers and acts of devotion that their children learn... Without mothers, not only would there be no new faithful, but the faith itself would lose a good part of its simple and profound warmth... Dear mothers: thank you! Thank you for what you are in your family and for what you give to the Church and the world".[193]

---

[190] JOHN PAUL II, Catechesis (12 March 1980), 2: Insegnamenti III/1 (1980), 542.

[191] Cf. ID., Apostolic Letter Mulieris Dignitatem (15 August 1988), 30-31: AAS 80 (1988), 1726-1729.

[192] Catechesis (7 January 2015): L'Osservatore Romano, 7-8 January 2015, p. 8.

[193] Ibid.

175. A mother who watches over her child with tenderness and compassion helps him or her to grow in confidence and to experience that the world is a good and welcoming place. This helps the child to grow in self-esteem and, in turn, to develop a capacity for intimacy and empathy. A father, for his part, helps the child to perceive the limits of life, to be open to the challenges of the wider world, and to see the need for hard work and strenuous effort. A father possessed of a clear and serene masculine identity who demonstrates affection and concern for his wife is just as necessary as a caring mother. There can be a certain flexibility of roles and responsibilities, depending on the concrete circumstances of each particular family. But the clear and well-defined presence of both figures, female and male, creates the environment best suited to the growth of the child.

176. We often hear that ours is "a society without fathers". In Western culture, the father figure is said to be symbolically absent, missing or vanished. Manhood itself seems to be called into question. The result has been an understandable confusion. "At first, this was perceived as a liberation: liberation from the father as master, from the father as the representative of a law imposed from without, from the father as the arbiter of his children's happiness and an obstacle to the emancipation and autonomy of young people. In some homes authoritarianism once reigned and, at times, even oppression".[194] Yet, "as often happens, one goes from one extreme to the other. In our day, the problem no longer seems to be the overbearing presence of the father so much as his absence, his not being there. Fathers are often so caught up in themselves and their work, and at times in their own self-fulfilment, that they neglect their families. They leave the little ones and the young to themselves".[195] The presence of the father, and hence his authority, is also impacted by the amount of time given over to the communications and entertainment media. Nowadays authority is often considered suspect and adults treated with impertinence. They themselves become uncertain and so fail to offer sure and solid guidance to their children. A reversal of the roles of parents and children is unhealthy, since it hinders the proper process of development

---

[194] *Catechesis* (28 January 2015): *L'Osservatore Romano*, 29 January 2015, p. 8.
[195] *Ibid.*

that children need to experience, and it denies them the love and guidance needed to mature.[196]

177. God sets the father in the family so that by the gifts of his masculinity he can be "close to his wife and share everything, joy and sorrow, hope and hardship. And to be close to his children as they grow - when they play and when they work, when they are carefree and when they are distressed, when they are talkative and when they are silent, when they are daring and when they are afraid, when they stray and when they get back on the right path. To be a father who is always present. When I say 'present', I do not mean 'controlling'. Fathers who are too controlling overshadow their children, they don't let them develop".[197] Some fathers feel they are useless or unnecessary, but the fact is that "children need to find a father waiting for them when they return home with their problems. They may try hard not to admit it, not to show it, but they need it".[198] It is not good for children to lack a father and to grow up before they are ready.

AN EXPANDING FRUITFULNESS

178. Some couples are unable to have children. We know that this can be a cause of real suffering for them. At the same time, we know that "marriage was not instituted solely for the procreation of children... Even in cases where, despite the intense desire of the spouses, there are no children, marriage still retains its character of being a whole manner and communion of life, and preserves its value and indissolubility".[199] So too, "motherhood is not a solely biological reality, but is expressed in diverse ways".[200]

179. Adoption is a very generous way to become parents. I encourage those who cannot have children to expand their marital love to embrace those who lack a proper family situation. They will never regret having

---

[196] Cf. *Relatio Finalis* 2015, 28.

[197] *Catechesis* (4 February 2015), *L'Osservatore Romano*, 5 February 2015, p. 8.

[198] *Ibid.*

[199] Second Vatican Ecumenical Council, Pastoral Constitution on the Church in the Modern World *Gaudium et Spes*, 50.

[200] Fifth General Conference of the Latin American and Caribbean Bishops, *Aparecida Document* (29 June 2007), No. 457.

been generous. Adopting a child is an act of love, offering the gift of a family to someone who has none. It is important to insist that legislation help facilitate the adoption process, above all in the case of unwanted children, in order to prevent their abortion or abandonment. Those who accept the challenge of adopting and accepting someone unconditionally and gratuitously become channels of God's love. For he says, "Even if your mother forgets you, I will not forget you" (*Is* 49:15).

180. "The choice of adoption and foster care expresses a particular kind of fruitfulness in the marriage experience, and not only in cases of infertility. In the light of those situations where a child is desired at any cost, as a right for one's self-fulfilment, adoption and foster care, correctly understood, manifest an important aspect of parenting and the raising of children. They make people aware that children, whether natural, adoptive or taken in foster care, are persons in their own right who need to be accepted, loved and cared for, and not just brought into this world. The best interests of the child should always underlie any decision in adoption and foster care".[201] On the other hand, "the trafficking of children between countries and continents needs to be prevented by appropriate legislative action and state control".[202]

181. We also do well to remember that procreation and adoption are not the only ways of experiencing the fruitfulness of love. Even large families are called to make their mark on society, finding other expressions of fruitfulness that in some way prolong the love that sustains them. Christian families should never forget that "faith does not remove us from the world, but draws us more deeply into it... Each of us, in fact, has a special role in preparing for the coming of God's kingdom in our world".[203] Families should not see themselves as a refuge from society, but instead go forth from their homes in a spirit of solidarity with others. In this way, they become a hub for integrating persons into society and a point of contact between the public and private spheres. Married couples should have a

---

[201] *Relatio Finalis* 2015, 65.

[202] *Ibid.*

[203] *Address at the Meeting with Families in Manila* (16 January 2015): AAS 107 (2015), 178.

clear awareness of their social obligations. With this, their affection does not diminish but is flooded with new light. As the poet says:

Your hands are my caress,
The harmony that fills my days.
I love you because your hands
Work for justice.

If I love you, it is because you are
My love, my companion and my all,
And on the street, side by side,
We are much more than just two.[204]

182. No family can be fruitful if it sees itself as overly different or "set apart". To avoid this risk, we should remember that Jesus' own family, so full of grace and wisdom, did not appear unusual or different from others. That is why people found it hard to acknowledge Jesus' wisdom: "Where did this man get all this? Is not this the carpenter, the son of Mary?" (*Mk* 6:2-3). "Is this not the carpenter's son?" (*Mt* 13: 55). These questions make it clear that theirs was an ordinary family, close to others, a normal part of the community. Jesus did not grow up in a narrow and stifling relationship with Mary and Joseph, but readily interacted with the wider family, the relatives of his parents and their friends. This explains how, on returning from Jerusalem, Mary and Joseph could imagine for a whole day that the twelve-year-old Jesus was somewhere in the caravan, listening to people's stories and sharing their concerns: "Supposing him to be in the group of travellers, they went a day's journey" (*Lk* 2:44). Still, some Christian families, whether because of the language they use, the way they act or treat others, or their constant harping on the same two or three issues, end up being seen as remote and not really a part of the community. Even their relatives feel looked down upon or judged by them.

183. A married couple who experience the power of love know that this love is called to bind the wounds of the outcast, to foster a culture of

---

[204] Mario Benedetti, "Te Quiero", in *Poemas de otros*, Buenos Aires 1993, 316: "*"Tus manos son mi caricia / mis acordes cotidianos / te quiero porque tus manos / trabajan por la justicia. // Si te quiero es porque sos / mi amor mi cómplice y todo / y en la calle codo a codo / somos mucho más que dos.*

encounter and to fight for justice. God has given the family the job of "domesticating" the world[205] and helping each person to see fellow human beings as brothers and sisters. "An attentive look at the everyday life of today's men and women immediately shows the omnipresent need for a healthy injection of family spirit… Not only is the organization of ordinary life increasingly thwarted by a bureaucracy completely removed from fundamental human bonds, but even social and political mores show signs of degradation".[206] For their part, open and caring families find a place for the poor and build friendships with those less fortunate than themselves. In their efforts to live according to the Gospel, they are mindful of Jesus' words: "As you did it to one of the least of these my brethren, you did it to me (*Mt* 25:40)". In a very real way, their lives express what is asked of us all: "When you give a dinner or a banquet, do not invite your friends or your brothers or your kinsmen or rich neighbours, lest they also invite you in return, and you be repaid. But when you give a feast, invite the poor, the maimed, the lame, the blind, and you will be blessed" (*Lk* 14:12-14). You will be blessed! Here is the secret to a happy family.

184. By their witness as well as their words, families speak to others of Jesus. They pass on the faith, they arouse a desire for God and they reflect the beauty of the Gospel and its way of life. Christian marriages thus enliven society by their witness of fraternity, their social concern, their outspokenness on behalf of the underprivileged, their luminous faith and their active hope. Their fruitfulness expands and in countless ways makes God's love present in society.

Discerning the body

185. Along these same lines, we do well to take seriously a biblical text usually interpreted outside of its context or in a generic sense, with the risk of overlooking its immediate and direct meaning, which is markedly social. I am speaking of *1 Cor* 11:17-34, where Saint Paul faces a shameful situation in the community. The wealthier members tended to discriminate against the poorer ones, and this carried over even to the *agape* meal that

---

[205] Cf. *Catechesis* (16 September 2015): *L'Osservatore Romano*, 17 September 2015, p. 8.

[206] *Catechesis* (7 October 2015): *L'Osservatore Romano*, 9 October 2015, p. 8.

accompanied the celebration of the Eucharist. While the rich enjoyed their food, the poor looked on and went hungry: "One is hungry and another is drunk. Do you not have houses to eat and drink in? Or do you despise the Church of God and humiliate those who have nothing?" (vv. 21-22).

186. The Eucharist demands that we be members of the one body of the Church. Those who approach the Body and Blood of Christ may not wound that same Body by creating scandalous distinctions and divisions among its members. This is what it means to "discern" the body of the Lord, to acknowledge it with faith and charity both in the sacramental signs and in the community; those who fail to do so eat and drink judgement against themselves (cf. v. 29). The celebration of the Eucharist thus becomes a constant summons for everyone "to examine himself or herself " (v. 28), to open the doors of the family to greater fellowship with the underprivileged, and in this way to receive the sacrament of that eucharistic love which makes us one body. We must not forget that "the 'mysticism' of the sacrament has a social character".[207] When those who receive it turn a blind eye to the poor and suffering, or consent to various forms of division, contempt and inequality, the Eucharist is received unworthily. On the other hand, families who are properly disposed and receive the Eucharist regularly, reinforce their desire for fraternity, their social consciousness and their commitment to those in need.

LIFE IN THE WIDER FAMILY

187. The nuclear family needs to interact with the wider family made up of parents, aunts and uncles, cousins and even neighbours. This greater family may have members who require assistance, or at least companionship and affection, or consolation amid suffering.[208] The individualism so prevalent today can lead to creating small nests of security, where others are perceived as bothersome or a threat. Such isolation, however, cannot offer greater peace or happiness; rather, it straitens the heart of a family and makes its life all the more narrow.

---

[207] BENEDICT XVI, Encyclical Letter *Deus Caritas Est* (25 December 2005), 14: AAS 98 (2006), 228.

[208] Cf. *Relatio Finalis* 2015, 11.

Being sons and daughters

188. First, let us think of our parents. Jesus told the Pharisees that abandoning one's parents is contrary to God's law (cf. *Mk* 7:8-13). We do well to remember that each of us is a son or daughter. "Even if one becomes an adult, or an elderly person, even if one becomes a parent, if one occupies a position of responsibility, underneath all of this is still the identity of a child. We are all sons and daughters. And this always brings us back to the fact that we did not give ourselves life but that we received it. The great gift of life is the first gift that we received".[209]

189. Hence, "the fourth commandment asks children… to honour their father and mother (cf. *Ex* 20:12). This commandment comes immediately after those dealing with God himself. Indeed, it has to do with something sacred, something divine, something at the basis of every other kind of human respect. The biblical formulation of the fourth commandment goes on to say: 'that your days may be long in the land which the Lord your God gives you'. The virtuous bond between generations is the guarantee of the future, and is the guarantee of a truly humane society. A society with children who do not honour parents is a society without honour… It is a society destined to be filled with surly and greedy young people".[210]

190. There is, however, another side to the coin. As the word of God tells us, "a man leaves his father and his mother" (*Gen* 2:24). This does not always happen, and a marriage is hampered by the failure to make this necessary sacrifice and surrender. Parents must not be abandoned or ignored, but marriage itself demands that they be "left", so that the new home will be a true hearth, a place of security, hope and future plans, and the couple can truly become "one flesh" (*ibid.*). In some marriages, one spouse keeps secrets from the other, confiding them instead to his or her parents. As a result, the opinions of their parents become more important than the feelings and opinions of their spouse. This situation cannot go on for long, and even if it takes time, both spouses need to make the effort to grow in trust and communication. Marriage challenges husbands and wives to find new ways of being sons and daughters.

---

[209] *Catechesis* (18 March 2015): *L'Osservatore Romano*, 19 March 2015, p. 8.

[210] *Catechesis* (11 February 2015): *L'Osservatore Romano*, 12 February 2015, p. 8.

The elderly

191. "Do not cast me off in the time of old age; forsake me not when my strength is spent" (*Ps* 71:9). This is the plea of the elderly, who fear being forgotten and rejected. Just as God asks us to be his means of hearing the cry of the poor, so too he wants us to hear the cry of the elderly.[211] This represents a challenge to families and communities, since "the Church cannot and does not want to conform to a mentality of impatience, and much less of indifference and contempt, towards old age. We must reawaken the collective sense of gratitude, of appreciation, of hospitality, which makes the elderly feel like a living part of the community. Our elderly are men and women, fathers and mothers, who came before us on our own road, in our own house, in our daily battle for a worthy life".[212] Indeed, "how I would like a Church that challenges the throw-away culture by the overflowing joy of a new embrace between young and old!"[213]

192. Saint John Paul II asked us to be attentive to the role of the elderly in our families, because there are cultures which, "especially in the wake of disordered industrial and urban development, have both in the past and in the present set the elderly aside in unacceptable ways".[214] The elderly help us to appreciate "the continuity of the generations", by their "charism of bridging the gap".[215] Very often it is grandparents who ensure that the most important values are passed down to their grandchildren, and "many people can testify that they owe their initiation into the Christian life to their grandparents".[216] Their words, their affection or simply their presence help children to realize that history did not begin with them, that they are now part of an age-old pilgrimage and that they need to respect all that came before them. Those who would break all ties with the past will surely find it difficult to build stable relationships and to

[211] Cf. *Relatio Finalis* 2015, 17-18.

[212] *Catechesis* (4 March 2015): *L'Osservatore Romano*, 5 March 2015, p. 8.

[213] *Catechesis* (11 March 2015): *L'Osservatore Romano*, 12 March 2015, p. 8.

[214] Apostolic Exhortation *Familiaris Consortio*, 27 (22 November 1981): AAS 74 (1982), 113.

[215] ID., *Address to Participants in the "International Forum on Active Aging"* (5 September 1980), 5: *Insegnamenti* III/2 (1980), 539.

[216] *Relatio Finalis* 2015, 18.

realize that reality is bigger than they are. "Attention to the elderly makes the difference in a society. Does a society show concern for the elderly? Does it make room for the elderly? Such a society will move forward if it respects the wisdom of the elderly".[217]

193. The lack of historical memory is a serious shortcoming in our society. A mentality that can only say, "Then was then, now is now", is ultimately immature. Knowing and judging past events is the only way to build a meaningful future. Memory is necessary for growth: "Recall the former days" (*Heb* 10:32). Listening to the elderly tell their stories is good for children and young people; it makes them feel connected to the living history of their families, their neighbourhoods and their country. A family that fails to respect and cherish its grandparents, who are its living memory, is already in decline, whereas a family that remembers has a future. "A society that has no room for the elderly or discards them because they create problems, has a deadly virus";[218] "it is torn from its roots".[219] Our contemporary experience of being orphans as a result of cultural discontinuity, uprootedness and the collapse of the certainties that shape our lives, challenges us to make our families places where children can sink roots in the rich soil of a collective history.

Being brothers and sisters

194. Relationships between brothers and sisters deepen with the passing of time, and "the bond of fraternity that forms in the family between children, if consolidated by an educational atmosphere of openness to others, is a great school of freedom and peace. In the family, we learn how to live as one. Perhaps we do not always think about this, but the family itself introduces fraternity into the world. From this initial experience of fraternity, nourished by affection and education at home, the style of fraternity radiates like a promise upon the whole of society".[220]

---

[217] *Catechesis* (4 March 2015): *L'Osservatore Romano*, 5 March 2015, p. 8.

[218] *Ibid.*

[219] *Address at the Meeting with the Elderly* (28 September 2014): *L'Osservatore Romano*, 29-30 September 2014, p. 7.

[220] *Catechesis* (18 February 2015): *L'Osservatore Romano*, 19 February 2015, p. 8.

195. Growing up with brothers and sisters makes for a beautiful experience of caring for and helping one another. For "fraternity in families is especially radiant when we see the care, the patience, the affection that surround the little brother or sister who is frail, sick or disabled".[221] It must be acknowledged that "having a brother or a sister who loves you is a profound, precious and unique experience".[222] Children do need to be patiently taught to treat one another as brothers and sisters. This training, at times quite demanding, is a true school of socialization. In some countries, where it has become quite common to have only one child, the experience of being a brother or sister is less and less common. When it has been possible to have only one child, ways have to be found to ensure that he or she does not grow up alone or isolated.

A big heart

196. In addition to the small circle of the couple and their children, there is the larger family, which cannot be overlooked. Indeed, "the love between husband and wife and, in a derivative and broader way, the love between members of the same family - between parents and children, brothers and sisters and relatives and members of the household - is given life and sustenance by an unceasing inner dynamism leading the family to ever deeper and more intense communion, which is the foundation and soul of the community of marriage and the family".[223] Friends and other families are part of this larger family, as well as communities of families who support one another in their difficulties, their social commitments and their faith.

197. This larger family should provide love and support to teenage mothers, children without parents, single mothers left to raise children, persons with disabilities needing particular affection and closeness, young people struggling with addiction, the unmarried, separated or widowed who are alone, and the elderly and infirm who lack the support of their children. It should also embrace "even those who have made

---

[221] *Ibid.*

[222] *Ibid.*

[223] JOHN PAUL II, Apostolic Exhortation *Familiaris Consortio* (22 November 1981), 18: AAS 74 (1982), 101.

shipwreck of their lives".[224] This wider family can help make up for the shortcomings of parents, detect and report possible situations in which children suffer violence and even abuse, and provide wholesome love and family stability in cases when parents prove incapable of this.

198. Finally, we cannot forget that this larger family includes fathers-in-law, mothers-in-law and all the relatives of the couple. One particularly delicate aspect of love is learning not to view these relatives as somehow competitors, threats or intruders. The conjugal union demands respect for their traditions and customs, an effort to understand their language and to refrain from criticism, caring for them and cherishing them while maintaining the legitimate privacy and independence of the couple. Being willing to do so is also an exquisite expression of generous love for one's spouse.

---

[224] *Catechesis* (7 October 2015): *L'Osservatore Romano*, 8 October 2015), p. 8.

CHAPTER SIX
SOME PASTORAL PERSPECTIVES

199. The dialogue that took place during the Synod raised the need for new pastoral methods. I will attempt to mention some of these in a very general way. Different communities will have to devise more practical and effective initiatives that respect both the Church's teaching and local problems and needs. Without claiming to present a pastoral plan for the family, I would now like to reflect on some more significant pastoral challenges.

PROCLAIMING THE GOSPEL OF THE FAMILY TODAY

200. The Synod Fathers emphasized that Christian families, by the grace of the sacrament of matrimony, are the principal agents of the family apostolate, above all through "their joy-filled witness as domestic churches".[225] Consequently, "it is important that people experience the Gospel of the family as a joy that 'fills hearts and lives', because in Christ we have been 'set free from sin, sorrow, inner emptiness and loneliness' (*Evangelii Gaudium*, 1). As in the parable of the sower (cf. *Mt* 13:3-9), we are called to help sow seeds; the rest is God's work. Nor must we forget that, in her teaching on the family, the Church is a sign of contradiction".[226] Married couples are grateful that their pastors uphold the high ideal of a love that is strong, solid, enduring and capable of sustaining them through whatever trials they may have to face. The Church wishes, with humility and compassion, to reach out to families and "to help each family to discover the best way to overcome any obstacles it encounters".[227] It is not enough to show generic concern for the family in pastoral planning. Enabling families to take up their role as active agents of the family apostolate calls for "an effort at evangelization and catechesis inside the family".[228]

---

[225] *Relatio Synodi* 2014, 30.

[226] *Ibid.*, 31.

[227] *Relatio Finalis* 2015, 56.

[228] *Ibid.*, 89.

201. "This effort calls for missionary conversion by everyone in the Church, that is, one that is not content to proclaim a merely theoretical message without connection to people's real problems".[229] Pastoral care for families "needs to make it clear that the Gospel of the family responds to the deepest expectations of the human person: a response to each one's dignity and fulfilment in reciprocity, communion and fruitfulness. This consists not merely in presenting a set of rules, but in proposing values that are clearly needed today, even in the most secularized of countries".[230] The Synod Fathers also "highlighted the fact that evangelization needs unambiguously to denounce cultural, social, political and economic factors - such as the excessive importance given to market logic - that prevent authentic family life and lead to discrimination, poverty, exclusion, and violence. Consequently, dialogue and co-operation need to be fostered with societal structures and encouragement given to lay people who are involved, as Christians, in the cultural and socio-political fields".[231]

202. "The main contribution to the pastoral care of families is offered by the parish, which is the family of families, where small communities, ecclesial movements and associations live in harmony".[232] Along with a pastoral outreach aimed specifically at families, this shows the need for "a more adequate formation... of priests, deacons, men and women religious, catechists and other pastoral workers".[233] In the replies given to the worldwide consultation, it became clear that ordained ministers often lack the training needed to deal with the complex problems currently facing families. The experience of the broad oriental tradition of a married clergy could also be drawn upon.

203. Seminarians should receive a more extensive interdisciplinary, and not merely doctrinal, formation in the areas of engagement and marriage. Their training does not always allow them to explore their own psychological and affective background and experiences. Some come

---

[229] *Relatio Synodi* 2014, 32.

[230] *Ibid.*, 33.

[231] *Ibid.*, 38.

[232] *Relatio Finalis* 2015, 77.

[233] *Ibid.*, 61.

from troubled families, with absent parents and a lack of emotional stability. There is a need to ensure that the formation process can enable them to attain the maturity and psychological balance needed for their future ministry. Family bonds are essential for reinforcing healthy self-esteem. It is important for families to be part of the seminary process and priestly life, since they help to reaffirm these and to keep them well grounded in reality. It is helpful for seminarians to combine time in the seminary with time spent in parishes. There they can have greater contact with the concrete realities of family life, since in their future ministry they will largely be dealing with families. "The presence of lay people, families and especially the presence of women in priestly formation, promotes an appreciation of the diversity and complementarity of the different vocations in the Church".[234]

204. The response to the consultation also insisted on the need for training lay leaders who can assist in the pastoral care of families, with the help of teachers and counsellors, family and community physicians, social workers, juvenile and family advocates, and drawing upon the contributions of psychology, sociology, marital therapy and counselling. Professionals, especially those with practical experience, help keep pastoral initiatives grounded in the real situations and concrete concerns of families. "Courses and programmes, planned specifically for pastoral workers, can be of assistance by integrating the premarital preparation programme into the broader dynamic of ecclesial life".[235] Good pastoral training is important "especially in light of particular emergency situations arising from cases of domestic violence and sexual abuse".[236] All this in no way diminishes, but rather complements, the fundamental value of spiritual direction, the rich spiritual treasures of the Church, and sacramental Reconciliation.

---

[234] *Ibid.*

[235] *Ibid.*

[236] *Ibid.*

PREPARING ENGAGED COUPLES FOR MARRIAGE

205. The Synod Fathers stated in a number of ways that we need to help young people discover the dignity and beauty of marriage.[237] They should be helped to perceive the attraction of a complete union that elevates and perfects the social dimension of existence, gives sexuality its deepest meaning, and benefits children by offering them the best context for their growth and development.

206. "The complexity of today's society and the challenges faced by the family require a greater effort on the part of the whole Christian community in preparing those who are about to be married. The importance of the virtues needs to be included. Among these, chastity proves invaluable for the genuine growth of love between persons. In this regard, the Synod Fathers agreed on the need to involve the entire community more extensively by stressing the witness of families themselves and by grounding marriage preparation in the process of Christian initiation by bringing out the connection between marriage, baptism and the other sacraments. The Fathers also spoke of the need for specific programmes of marriage preparation aimed at giving couples a genuine experience of participation in ecclesial life and a complete introduction to various aspects of family life".[238]

207. I encourage Christian communities to recognize the great benefit that they themselves receive from supporting engaged couples as they grow in love. As the Italian bishops have observed, those couples are "a valuable resource because, as they sincerely commit themselves to grow in love and self-giving, they can help renew the fabric of the whole ecclesial body. Their special form of friendship can prove contagious and foster the growth of friendship and fraternity in the Christian community of which they are a part".[239] There are a number of legitimate ways to structure programmes of marriage preparation, and each local Church will discern how best to provide a suitable formation without distancing young people

---

[237] Cf. *Relatio Synodi* 2014, 26.

[238] *Ibid.*, 39.

[239] ITALIAN BISHOPS' CONFERENCE, Episcopal Commission on Family and Life, *Orientamenti pastorali sulla preparazione al matrimonio e alla famiglia* (22 October 2012), 1.

from the sacrament. They do not need to be taught the entire *Catechism* or overwhelmed with too much information. Here too, "it is not great knowledge, but rather the ability to feel and relish things interiorly that contents and satisfies the soul".[240] Quality is more important than quantity, and priority should be given - along with a renewed proclamation of the kerygma - to an attractive and helpful presentation of information that can help couples to live the rest of their lives together "with great courage and generosity".[241] Marriage preparation should be a kind of "initiation" to the sacrament of matrimony, providing couples with the help they need to receive the sacrament worthily and to make a solid beginning of life as a family.

208. With the help of missionary families, the couple's own families and a variety of pastoral resources, ways should also be found to offer a remote preparation that, by example and good advice, can help their love to grow and mature. Discussion groups and optional talks on a variety of topics of genuine interest to young people can also prove helpful. All the same, some individual meetings remain essential, since the primary objective is to help each to learn how to love this very real person with whom he or she plans to share his or her whole life. Learning to love someone does not happen automatically, nor can it be taught in a workshop just prior to the celebration of marriage. For every couple, marriage preparation begins at birth. What they received from their family should prepare them to know themselves and to make a full and definitive commitment. Those best prepared for marriage are probably those who learned what Christian marriage is from their own parents, who chose each other unconditionally and daily renew this decision. In this sense, pastoral initiatives aimed at helping married couples to grow in love and in the Gospel of the family also help their children, by preparing them for their future married life. Nor should we underestimate the pastoral value of traditional religious practices. To give just one example: I think of Saint Valentine's Day; in some countries, commercial interests are quicker to see the potential of this celebration than are we in the Church.

---

[240] IGNATIUS OF LOYOLA, *Spiritual Exercises*, Annotation 2.

[241] *Ibid.*, Annotation 5.

209. The timely preparation of engaged couples by the parish community should also assist them to recognize eventual problems and risks. In this way, they can come to realize the wisdom of breaking off a relationship whose failure and painful aftermath can be foreseen. In their initial enchantment with one another, couples can attempt to conceal or relativize certain things and to avoid disagreements; only later do problems surface. For this reason, they should be strongly encouraged to discuss what each expects from marriage, what they understand by love and commitment, what each wants from the other and what kind of life they would like to build together. Such discussions would help them to see if they in fact have little in common and to realize that mutual attraction alone will not suffice to keep them together. Nothing is more volatile, precarious and unpredictable than desire. The decision to marry should never be encouraged unless the couple has discerned deeper reasons that will ensure a genuine and stable commitment.

210. In any event, if one partner clearly recognizes the other's weak points, he or she needs to have a realistic trust in the possibility of helping to develop the good points that counterbalance them, and in this way to foster their human growth. This entails a willingness to face eventual sacrifices, problems and situations of conflict; it demands a firm resolve to be ready for this. Couples need to be able to detect danger signals in their relationship and to find, before the wedding, effective ways of responding to them. Sadly, many couples marry without really knowing one another. They have enjoyed each other's company and done things together, but without facing the challenge of revealing themselves and coming to know who the other person truly is.

211. Both short-term and long-term marriage preparation should ensure that the couple do not view the wedding ceremony as the end of the road, but instead embark upon marriage as a lifelong calling based on a firm and realistic decision to face all trials and difficult moments together. The pastoral care of engaged and married couples should be centred on the marriage bond, assisting couples not only to deepen their love but also to overcome problems and difficulties. This involves not only helping them to accept the Church's teaching and to have recourse to

her valuable resources, but also offering practical programmes, sound advice, proven strategies and psychological guidance. All this calls for a pedagogy of love, attuned to the feelings and needs of young people and capable of helping them to grow interiorly. Marriage preparation should also provide couples with the names of places, people and services to which they can turn for help when problems arise. It is also important to remind them of the availability of the sacrament of Reconciliation, which allows them to bring their sins and past mistakes, and their relationship itself, before God, and to receive in turn his merciful forgiveness and healing strength.

The preparation of the celebration

212. Short-term preparations for marriage tend to be concentrated on invitations, clothes, the party and any number of other details that tend to drain not only the budget but energy and joy as well. The spouses come to the wedding ceremony exhausted and harried, rather than focused and ready for the great step that they are about to take. The same kind of preoccupation with a big celebration also affects certain de facto unions; because of the expenses involved, the couple, instead of being concerned above all with their love and solemnizing it in the presence of others, never get married. Here let me say a word to fiancés. Have the courage to be different. Don't let yourselves get swallowed up by a society of consumption and empty appearances. What is important is the love you share, strengthened and sanctified by grace. You are capable of opting for a more modest and simple celebration in which love takes precedence over everything else. Pastoral workers and the entire community can help make this priority the norm rather than the exception.

213. In their preparation for marriage, the couple should be encouraged to make the liturgical celebration a profound personal experience and to appreciate the meaning of each of its signs. In the case of two baptized persons, the commitment expressed by the words of consent and the bodily union that consummates the marriage can only be seen as signs of the covenantal love and union between the incarnate Son of God and his Church. In the baptized, words and signs become an eloquent language of faith. The body, created with a God-given meaning, "becomes the

language of the ministers of the sacrament, aware that in the conjugal pact there is expressed and realized the mystery that has its origin in God himself".[242]

214. At times, the couple does not grasp the theological and spiritual import of the words of consent, which illuminate the meaning of all the signs that follow. It needs to be stressed that these words cannot be reduced to the present; they involve a totality that includes the future: "until death do us part". The content of the words of consent makes it clear that "freedom and fidelity are not opposed to one another; rather, they are mutually supportive, both in interpersonal and social relationships. Indeed, let us consider the damage caused, in our culture of global communication, by the escalation of unkept promises... Honouring one's word, fidelity to one's promises: these are things that cannot be bought and sold. They cannot be compelled by force or maintained without sacrifice".[243]

215. The Kenyan Bishops have observed that "many [young people] concentrate on their wedding day and forget the life-long commitment they are about to enter into".[244] They need to be encouraged to see the sacrament not as a single moment that then becomes a part of the past and its memories, but rather as a reality that permanently influences the whole of married life.[245] The procreative meaning of sexuality, the language of the body, and the signs of love shown throughout married life, all become an "uninterrupted continuity of liturgical language" and "conjugal life becomes in a certain sense liturgical".[246]

216. The couple can also meditate on the biblical readings and the meaningfulness of the rings they will exchange and the other signs that are part of the rite. Nor would it be good for them to arrive at the wedding without ever having prayed together, one for the other, to seek God's help in remaining faithful and generous, to ask the Lord together

---

[242] JOHN PAUL II, *Catechesis* (27 June 1984), 4: *Insegnamenti* VII/1 (1984), 1941.

[243] *Catechesis* (21 October 2015): *L'Osservatore Romano*, 22 October 2015, p. 12.

[244] KENYA CONFERENCE OF CATHOLIC BISHOPS, *Lenten Message* (18 February 2015).

[245] Cf. PIUS XI, Encyclical Letter *Casti Connubii* (31 December 1930): AAS 22 (1930), 583.

[246] JOHN PAUL II, *Catechesis* (4 July 1984), 3, 6: *Insegnamenti* VII/2 (1984), pp. 9, 10.

what he wants of them, and to consecrate their love before an image of the Virgin Mary. Those who help prepare them for marriage should help them experience these moments of prayer that can prove so beneficial. "The marriage liturgy is a unique event, which is both a family and a community celebration. The first signs of Jesus were performed at the wedding feast of Cana. The good wine, resulting from the Lord's miracle that brought joy to the beginning of a new family, is the new wine of Christ's covenant with the men and women of every age... Frequently, the celebrant speaks to a congregation that includes people who seldom participate in the life of the Church, or who are members of other Christian denominations or religious communities. The occasion thus provides a valuable opportunity to proclaim the Gospel of Christ".[247]

ACCOMPANYING THE FIRST YEARS OF MARRIED LIFE

217. It is important that marriage be seen as a matter of love, that only those who freely choose and love one another may marry. When love is merely physical attraction or a vague affection, spouses become particularly vulnerable once this affection wanes or physical attraction diminishes. Given the frequency with which this happens, it is all the more essential that couples be helped during the first years of their married life to enrich and deepen their conscious and free decision to have, hold and love one another for life. Often the engagement period is not long enough, the decision is precipitated for various reasons and, what is even more problematic, the couple themselves are insufficiently mature. As a result, the newly married couple need to complete a process that should have taken place during their engagement.

218. Another great challenge of marriage preparation is to help couples realize that marriage is not something that happens once for all. Their union is real and irrevocable, confirmed and consecrated by the sacrament of matrimony. Yet in joining their lives, the spouses assume an active and creative role in a lifelong project. Their gaze now has to be directed to the future that, with the help of God's grace, they are daily called to build. For this very reason, neither spouse can expect the other to be perfect. Each

---

[247] *Relatio Finalis* 2015, 59.

must set aside all illusions and accept the other as he or she actually is: an unfinished product, needing to grow, a work in progress. A persistently critical attitude towards one's partner is a sign that marriage was not entered into as a project to be worked on together, with patience, understanding, tolerance and generosity. Slowly but surely, love will then give way to constant questioning and criticism, dwelling on each other's good and bad points, issuing ultimatums and engaging in competition and self-justification. The couple then prove incapable of helping one another to build a mature union. This fact needs to be realistically presented to newly married couples from the outset, so that they can grasp that the wedding is "just the beginning". By saying "I do", they embark on a journey that requires them to overcome all obstacles standing in the way of their reaching the goal. The nuptial blessing that they receive is a grace and an incentive for this journey. They can only benefit from sitting down and talking to one another about how, concretely, they plan to achieve their goal.

219. I recall an old saying: still water becomes stagnant and good for nothing. If, in the first years of marriage, a couple's experience of love grows stagnant, it loses the very excitement that should be its propelling force. Young love needs to keep dancing towards the future with immense hope. Hope is the leaven that, in those first years of engagement and marriage, makes it possible to look beyond arguments, conflicts and problems and to see things in a broader perspective. It harnesses our uncertainties and concerns so that growth can take place. Hope also bids us live fully in the present, giving our all to the life of the family, for the best way to prepare a solid future is to live well in the present.

220. This process occurs in various stages that call for generosity and sacrifice. The first powerful feelings of attraction give way to the realization that the other is now a part of my life. The pleasure of belonging to one another leads to seeing life as a common project, putting the other's happiness ahead of my own, and realizing with joy that this marriage enriches society. As love matures, it also learns to "negotiate". Far from anything selfish or calculating, such negotiation is an exercise of mutual love, an interplay of give and take, for the good of the family. At

each new stage of married life, there is a need to sit down and renegotiate agreements, so that there will be no winners and losers, but rather two winners. In the home, decisions cannot be made unilaterally, since each spouse shares responsibility for the family; yet each home is unique and each marriage will find an arrangement that works best.

221. Among the causes of broken marriages are unduly high expectations about conjugal life. Once it becomes apparent that the reality is more limited and challenging than one imagined, the solution is not to think quickly and irresponsibly about separation, but to come to the sober realization that married life is a process of growth, in which each spouse is God's means of helping the other to mature. Change, improvement, the flowering of the good qualities present in each person - all these are possible. Each marriage is a kind of "salvation history", which from fragile beginnings - thanks to God's gift and a creative and generous response on our part - grows over time into something precious and enduring. Might we say that the greatest mission of two people in love is to help one another become, respectively, more a man and more a woman? Fostering growth means helping a person to shape his or her own identity. Love is thus a kind of craftsmanship. When we read in the Bible about the creation of man and woman, we see God first forming Adam (cf. *Gen* 2:7); he realizes that something essential is lacking and so he forms Eve and then hears the man exclaim in amazement, "Yes, this one is just right for me!" We can almost hear the amazing dialogue that must have taken place when the man and the woman first encountered one another. In the life of married couples, even at difficult moments, one person can always surprise the other, and new doors can open for their relationship, as if they were meeting for the first time. At every new stage, they can keep "forming" one another. Love makes each wait for the other with the patience of a craftsman, a patience which comes from God.

222. The pastoral care of newly married couples must also involve encouraging them to be generous in bestowing life. "In accord with the personal and fully human character of conjugal love, family planning fittingly takes place as the result a consensual dialogue between the spouses, respect for times and consideration of the dignity of the partner.

In this sense, the teaching of the Encyclical *Humanae Vitae* (cf. 1014) and the Apostolic Exhortation *Familiaris Consortio* (cf. 14; 2835) ought to be taken up anew, in order to counter a mentality that is often hostile to life... Decisions involving responsible parenthood presupposes the formation of conscience, which is 'the most secret core and sanctuary of a person. There each one is alone with God, whose voice echoes in the depths of the heart' (*Gaudium et Spes*, 16). The more the couple tries to listen in conscience to God and his commandments (cf. *Rom* 2:15), and is accompanied spiritually, the more their decision will be profoundly free of subjective caprice and accommodation to prevailing social mores".[248] The clear teaching of the Second Vatican Council still holds: "[The couple] will make decisions by common counsel and effort. Let them thoughtfully take into account both their own welfare and that of their children, those already born and those which the future may bring. For this accounting they need to reckon with both the material and the spiritual conditions of the times as well as of their state in life. Finally, they should consult the interests of the family group, of temporal society and of the Church herself. The parents themselves and no one else should ultimately make this judgement in the sight of God".[249] Moreover, "the use of methods based on the 'laws of nature and the incidence of fertility' (*Humanae Vitae*, 11) are to be promoted, since 'these methods respect the bodies of the spouses, encourage tenderness between them and favour the education of an authentic freedom' (*Catechism of the Catholic Church*, 2370). Greater emphasis needs to be placed on the fact that children are a wonderful gift from God and a joy for parents and the Church. Through them, the Lord renews the world".[250]

Some resources

223. The Synod Fathers observed that "the initial years of marriage are a vital and sensitive period during which couples become more aware of the challenges and meaning of married life. Consequently, pastoral accompaniment needs to go beyond the actual celebration of the

---

[248] *Ibid.*, 63.

[249] SECOND VATICAN ECUMENICAL COUNCIL, Pastoral Constitution on the Church in the Modern World *Gaudium et Spes*, 50.

[250] *Relatio Finalis* 2015, 63.

sacrament (*Familiaris Consortio*, Part III). In this regard, experienced couples have an important role to play. The parish is a place where such experienced couples can help younger couples, with the eventual co-operation of associations, ecclesial movements and new communities. Young couples need to be encouraged to be essentially open to the great gift of children. Emphasis should also be given to the importance of family spirituality, prayer and participation in the Sunday Eucharist, and couples encouraged to meet regularly to promote growth in their spiritual life and solidarity in the concrete demands of life. Liturgies, devotional practices and the Eucharist celebrated for families, especially on the wedding anniversary, were mentioned as vital factors in fostering evangelization through the family".[251]

224. This process takes time. Love needs time and space; everything else is secondary. Time is needed to talk things over, to embrace leisurely, to share plans, to listen to one other and gaze in each other's eyes, to appreciate one another and to build a stronger relationship. Sometimes the frenetic pace of our society and the pressures of the workplace create problems. At other times, the problem is the lack of quality time together, sharing the same room without one even noticing the other. Pastoral workers and groups of married people should think of ways to help young or vulnerable couples to make the most of those moments, to be present to one another, even by sharing moments of meaningful silence.

225. Couples who have learned how to do this well can share some practical suggestions which they have found useful: planning free time together, moments of recreation with the children, different ways of celebrating important events, shared opportunities for spiritual growth. They can also provide resources that help young married couples to make those moments meaningful and loving, and thus to improve their communication. This is extremely important for the stage when the novelty of marriage has worn off. Once a couple no longer knows how to spend time together, one or both of them will end up taking refuge in gadgets, finding other commitments, seeking the embrace of another, or simply looking for ways to flee what has become an uncomfortable closeness.

---

[251] *Relatio Synodi* 2014, 40.

226. Young married couples should be encouraged to develop a routine that gives a healthy sense of closeness and stability through shared daily rituals. These could include a morning kiss, an evening blessing, waiting at the door to welcome each other home, taking trips together and sharing household chores. Yet it also helps to break the routine with a party, and to enjoy family celebrations of anniversaries and special events. We need these moments of cherishing God's gifts and renewing our zest for life. As long as we can celebrate, we are able to rekindle our love, to free it from monotony and to colour our daily routine with hope.

227. We pastors have to encourage families to grow in faith. This means encouraging frequent confession, spiritual direction and occasional retreats. It also means encouraging family prayer during the week, since "the family that prays together stays together". When visiting our people's homes, we should gather all the members of the family and briefly pray for one another, placing the family in the Lord's hands. It is also helpful to encourage each of the spouses to find time for prayer alone with God, since each has his or her secret crosses to bear. Why shouldn't we tell God our troubles and ask him to grant us the healing and help we need to remain faithful? The Synod Fathers noted that "the word of God is the source of life and spirituality for the family. All pastoral work on behalf of the family must allow people to be interiorly fashioned and formed as members of the domestic church through the Church's prayerful reading of sacred Scripture. The word of God is not only good news in a person's private life but also a criterion of judgement and a light in discerning the various challenges that married couples and families encounter".[252]

228. In some cases, one of the spouses is not baptized or does not want to practise the faith. This can make the other's desire to live and grow in the Christian life difficult and at times painful. Still, some common values can be found and these can be shared and relished. In any event, showing love for a spouse who is not a believer, bestowing happiness, soothing hurts and sharing life together represents a true path of sanctification. Love is always a gift of God. Wherever it is poured out,

---

[252] *Ibid.*, 34.

it makes its transforming presence felt, often in mysterious ways, even to the point that "the unbelieving husband is consecrated through his wife, and the unbelieving wife is consecrated through her husband" (*1 Cor* 7:14).

229. Parishes, movements, schools and other Church institutions can help in a variety of ways to support families and help them grow. These might include: meetings of couples living in the same neighbourhood, brief retreats for couples; talks by experts on concrete issues facing families, marriage counselling, home missionaries who help couples discuss their difficulties and desires, social services dealing with family problems like addiction, infidelity and domestic violence, programmes of spiritual growth, workshops for parents with troubled children and family meetings. The parish office should be prepared to deal helpfully and sensitively with family needs and be able to make referrals, when necessary, to those who can help. There is also the contribution made by groups of married couples that provide assistance as part of their commitment to service, prayer, formation and mutual support. Such groups enable couples to be generous, to assist other families and to share the faith; at the same time they strengthen marriages and help them to grow.

230. It is true that many couples, once married, drop out of the Christian community. Often, however, we ourselves do not take advantage of those occasions when they do return, to remind them of the beautiful ideal of Christian marriage and the support that our parishes can offer them. I think, for example, of the Baptism and First Holy Communion of their children, or the funerals or weddings of their relatives or friends. Almost all married couples reappear on these occasions, and we should take greater advantage of this. Another way of growing closer is by blessing homes or by bringing a pilgrim image of Our Lady to houses in the neighbourhood; this provides an opportunity for a pastoral conversation about the family's situation. It could also be helpful to ask older married couples to help younger couples in the neighbourhood by visiting them and offering guidance in the early years of marriage. Given the pace of life today, most couples cannot attend frequent meetings; still, we cannot restrict our pastoral outreach to small and select groups. Nowadays,

pastoral care for families has to be fundamentally missionary, going out to where people are. We can no longer be like a factory, churning out courses that for the most part are poorly attended.

CASTING LIGHT ON CRISES, WORRIES AND DIFFICULTIES

231. A word should also be said about those whose love, like a fine wine, has come into its own. Just as a good wine begins to "breathe" with time, so too the daily experience of fidelity gives married life richness and "body". Fidelity has to do with patience and expectation. Its joys and sacrifices bear fruit as the years go by and the couple rejoices to see their children's children. The love present from the beginning becomes more conscious, settled and mature as the couple discover each other anew day after day, year after year. Saint John of the Cross tells us that "old lovers are tried and true". They "are outwardly no longer afire with powerful emotions and impulses, but now taste the sweetness of the wine of love, well-aged and stored deep within their hearts".[253] Such couples have successfully overcome crises and hardships without fleeing from challenges or concealing problems.

The challenge of crises

232. The life of every family is marked by all kinds of crises, yet these are also part of its dramatic beauty. Couples should be helped to realize that surmounting a crisis need not weaken their relationship; instead, it can improve, settle and mature the wine of their union. Life together should not diminish but increase their contentment; every new step along the way can help couples find new ways to happiness. Each crisis becomes an apprenticeship in growing closer together or learning a little more about what it means to be married. There is no need for couples to resign themselves to an inevitable downward spiral or a tolerable mediocrity. On the contrary, when marriage is seen as a challenge that involves overcoming obstacles, each crisis becomes an opportunity to let the wine of their relationship age and improve. Couples will gain from receiving help in facing crises, meeting challenges and acknowledging them as part of family life. Experienced and trained couples should be open to offering

---

[253] *Cántico Espiritual* B, XXV, 11.

guidance, so the couples will not be unnerved by these crises or tempted to hasty decisions. Each crisis has a lesson to teach us; we need to learn how to listen for it with the ear of the heart.

233. Faced with a crisis, we tend first to react defensively, since we feel that we are losing control, or are somehow at fault, and this makes us uneasy. We resort to denying the problem, hiding or downplaying it, and hoping that it will go away. But this does not help; it only makes things worse, wastes energy and delays a solution. Couples grow apart and lose their ability to communicate. When problems are not dealt with, communication is the first thing to go. Little by little, the "the person I love" slowly becomes "my mate", then just "the father or mother of my children", and finally a stranger.

234. Crises need to be faced together. This is hard, since persons sometimes withdraw in order to avoid saying what they feel; they retreat into a craven silence. At these times, it becomes all the more important to create opportunities for speaking heart to heart. Unless a couple learns to do this, they will find it harder and harder as time passes. Communication is an art learned in moments of peace in order to be practised in moments of difficulty. Spouses need help in discovering their deepest thoughts and feelings and expressing them. Like childbirth, this is a painful process that brings forth a new treasure. The answers given to the pre-synodal consultation showed that most people in difficult or critical situations do not seek pastoral assistance, since they do not find it sympathetic, realistic or concerned for individual cases. This should spur us to try to approach marriage crises with greater sensitivity to their burden of hurt and anxiety.

235. Some crises are typical of almost every marriage. Newly married couples need to learn how to accept their differences and to disengage from their parents. The arrival of a child presents new emotional challenges. Raising small children necessitates a change of lifestyle, while the onset of adolescence causes strain, frustration and even tension between parents. An "empty nest" obliges a couple to redefine their relationship, while the need to care for ageing parents involves making

difficult decisions in their regard. All these are demanding situations that can cause apprehension, feelings of guilt, depression and fatigue, with serious repercussions on a marriage.

236. Then there are those personal crises that affect the life of couples, often involving finances, problems in the workplace, emotional, social and spiritual difficulties. Unexpected situations present themselves, disrupting family life and requiring a process of forgiveness and reconciliation. In resolving sincerely to forgive the other, each has to ask quietly and humbly if he or she has not somehow created the conditions that led to the other's mistakes. Some families break up when spouses engage in mutual recrimination, but "experience shows that with proper assistance and acts of reconciliation, through grace, a great percentage of troubled marriages find a solution in a satisfying manner. To know how to forgive and to feel forgiven is a basic experience in family life".[254] "The arduous art of reconciliation, which requires the support of grace, needs the generous co-operation of relatives and friends, and sometimes even outside help and professional assistance".[255]

237. It is becoming more and more common to think that, when one or both partners no longer feel fulfilled, or things have not turned out the way they wanted, sufficient reason exists to end the marriage. Were this the case, no marriage would last. At times, all it takes to decide that everything is over is a single instance of dissatisfaction, the absence of the other when he or she was most needed, wounded pride, or a vague fear. Inevitably, situations will arise involving human weakness and these can prove emotionally overwhelming. One spouse may not feel fully appreciated, or may be attracted to another person. Jealousy and tensions may emerge, or new interests that consume the other's time and attention. Physical changes naturally occur in everyone. These, and so many other things, rather than threatening love, are so many occasions for reviving and renewing it.

---

[254] *Relatio Synodi* 2014, 44.

[255] *Relatio Finalis* 2015, 81.

238. In such situations, some have the maturity needed to reaffirm their choice of the other as their partner on life's journey, despite the limitations of the relationship. They realistically accept that the other cannot fulfil all their cherished dreams. Persons like this avoid thinking of themselves as martyrs; they make the most of whatever possibilities family life gives them and they work patiently at strengthening the marriage bond. They realize, after all, that every crisis can be a new "yes", enabling love to be renewed, deepened and inwardly strengthened. When crises come, they are unafraid to get to the root of it, to renegotiate basic terms, to achieve a new equilibrium and to move forward together. With this kind of constant openness they are able to face any number of difficult situations. In any event, while realizing that reconciliation is a possibility, we also see that "what is urgently needed today is a ministry to care for those whose marital relationship has broken down".[256]

Old wounds

239. Understandably, families often experience problems when one of their members is emotionally immature because he or she still bears the scars of earlier experiences. An unhappy childhood or adolescence can breed personal crises that affect one's marriage. Were everyone mature and normal, crises would be less frequent or less painful. Yet the fact is that only in their forties do some people achieve a maturity that should have come at the end of adolescence. Some love with the selfish, capricious and self-centred love of a child: an insatiable love that screams or cries when it fails to get what it wants. Others love with an adolescent love marked by hostility, bitter criticism and the need to blame others; caught up in their own emotions and fantasies, such persons expect others to fill their emptiness and to satisfy their every desire.

240. Many people leave childhood without ever having felt unconditional love. This affects their ability to be trusting and open with others. A poor relationship with one's parents and siblings, if left unhealed, can re-emerge and hurt a marriage. Unresolved issues need to be dealt with and a process of liberation must take place. When problems emerge in a marriage, before

---

[256] *Ibid.*, 78.

important decisions are made it is important to ensure that each spouse has come to grips with his or her own history. This involves recognizing a need for healing, insistent prayer for the grace to forgive and be forgiven, a willingness to accept help, and the determination not to give up but to keep trying. A sincere self-examination will make it possible to see how one's own shortcomings and immaturity affect the relationship. Even if it seems clear that the other person is at fault, a crisis will never be overcome simply by expecting him or her to change. We also have to ask what in our own life needs to grow or heal if the conflict is to be resolved.

Accompaniment after breakdown and divorce

241. In some cases, respect for one's own dignity and the good of the children requires not giving in to excessive demands or preventing a grave injustice, violence or chronic ill-treatment. In such cases, "separation becomes inevitable. At times it even becomes morally necessary, precisely when it is a matter of removing the more vulnerable spouse or young children from serious injury due to abuse and violence, from humiliation and exploitation, and from disregard and indifference".[257] Even so, "separation must be considered as a last resort, after all other reasonable attempts at reconciliation have proved vain".[258]

242. The Synod Fathers noted that "special discernment is indispensable for the pastoral care of those who are separated, divorced or abandoned. Respect needs to be shown especially for the sufferings of those who have unjustly endured separation, divorce or abandonment, or those who have been forced by maltreatment from a husband or a wife to interrupt their life together. To forgive such an injustice that has been suffered is not easy, but grace makes this journey possible. Pastoral care must necessarily include efforts at reconciliation and mediation, through the establishment of specialized counselling centres in dioceses".[259] At the same time, "divorced people who have not remarried, and often bear witness to marital fidelity, ought to be encouraged to find in the Eucharist

---

[257] *Catechesis* (24 June 2015): *L'Osservatore Romano*, 25 June 2015, p. 8.

[258] JOHN PAUL II, Apostolic Exhortation *Familiaris Consortio* (22 November 1981), 83: AAS 74 (1982), 184.

[259] *Relatio Synodi* 2014, 47.

the nourishment they need to sustain them in their present state of life. The local community and pastors should accompany these people with solicitude, particularly when children are involved or when they are in serious financial difficulty".[260] Family breakdown becomes even more traumatic and painful in the case of the poor, since they have far fewer resources at hand for starting a new life. A poor person, once removed from a secure family environment, is doubly vulnerable to abandonment and possible harm.

243. It is important that the divorced who have entered a new union should be made to feel part of the Church. "They are not excommunicated" and they should not be treated as such, since they remain part of the ecclesial community.[261] These situations "require careful discernment and respectful accompaniment. Language or conduct that might lead them to feel discriminated against should be avoided, and they should be encouraged to participate in the life of the community. The Christian community's care of such persons is not to be considered a weakening of its faith and testimony to the indissolubility of marriage; rather, such care is a particular expression of its charity".[262]

244. A large number of Synod Fathers also "emphasized the need to make the procedure in cases of nullity more accessible and less time consuming, and, if possible, free of charge".[263] The slowness of the process causes distress and strain on the parties. My two recent documents dealing with this issue[264] have simplified the procedures for the declarations of matrimonial nullity. With these, I wished "to make clear that the bishop himself, in the Church over which he has been appointed shepherd and head, is by that very fact the judge of those faithful entrusted to his

---

[260] *Ibid.*, 50.

[261] *Catechesis* (5 August 2015): *L'Osservatore Romano*, 6 August 2015, p. 7.

[262] *Relatio Synodi* 2014, 51; cf. *Relatio Finalis* 2015, 84.

[263] *Ibid.*, 48.

[264] Motu Proprio *Mitis Iudex Dominus Iesus* (15 August 2015): *L'Osservatore Romano*, 9 September 2015, pp. 3-4; cf. Motu Proprio *Mitis et Misericors Iesus* (15 August 2015): *L'Osservatore Romano*, 9 September 2015, pp. 5-6.

care".[265] "The implementation of these documents is therefore a great responsibility for Ordinaries in dioceses, who are called upon to judge some cases themselves and, in every case, to ensure the faithful an easier access to justice. This involves preparing a sufficient staff, composed of clerics and lay persons who are primarily deputed to this ecclesial service. Information, counselling and mediation services associated with the family apostolate should also be made available to individuals who are separated or couples in crisis. These services could also include meeting with individuals in view of the preliminary inquiry of a matrimonial process (cf. *Mitis Iudex*, art. 2-3)".[266]

245. The Synod Fathers also pointed to "the consequences of separation or divorce on children, in every case the innocent victims of the situation".[267] Apart from every other consideration, the good of children should be the primary concern, and not overshadowed by any ulterior interest or objective. I make this appeal to parents who are separated: "Never ever, take your child hostage! You separated for many problems and reasons. Life gave you this trial, but your children should not have to bear the burden of this separation or be used as hostages against the other spouse. They should grow up hearing their mother speak well of their father, even though they are not together, and their father speak well of their mother".[268] It is irresponsible to disparage the other parent as a means of winning a child's affection, or out of revenge or self-justification. Doing so will affect the child's interior tranquillity and cause wounds hard to heal.

246. The Church, while appreciating the situations of conflict that are part of marriage, cannot fail to speak out on behalf of those who are most vulnerable: the children who often suffer in silence. Today, "despite our seemingly evolved sensibilities and all our refined psychological analyses, I ask myself if we are not becoming numb to the hurt in children's souls...

---

[265] Motu Proprio *Mitis Iudex Dominus Iesus* (15 August 2015), Preamble, III: *L'Osservatore Romano*, 9 September 2015, p. 3.

[266] *Relatio Finalis* 2015, 82.

[267] *Relatio Synodi* 2014, 47.

[268] *Catechesis* (20 May 2015): *L'Osservatore Romano*, 21 May 2015, p. 8.

Do we feel the immense psychological burden borne by children in families where the members mistreat and hurt one another, to the point of breaking the bonds of marital fidelity?"[269] Such harmful experiences do not help children to grow in the maturity needed to make definitive commitments. For this reason, Christian communities must not abandon divorced parents who have entered a new union, but should include and support them in their efforts to bring up their children. "How can we encourage those parents to do everything possible to raise their children in the Christian life, to give them an example of committed and practical faith, if we keep them at arm's length from the life of the community, as if they were somehow excommunicated? We must keep from acting in a way that adds even more to the burdens that children in these situations already have to bear!"[270] Helping heal the wounds of parents and supporting them spiritually is also beneficial for children, who need the familiar face of the Church to see them through this traumatic experience. Divorce is an evil and the increasing number of divorces is very troubling. Hence, our most important pastoral task with regard to families is to strengthen their love, helping to heal wounds and working to prevent the spread of this drama of our times.

Certain complex situations

247. "Issues involving mixed marriages require particular attention. Marriages between Catholics and other baptized persons 'have their own particular nature, but they contain numerous elements that could well be made good use of and developed, both for their intrinsic value and for the contribution that they can make to the ecumenical movement'. For this purpose, 'an effort should be made to establish cordial co-operation between the Catholic and the non-Catholic ministers from the time that preparations begin for the marriage and the wedding ceremony' (*Familiaris Consortio*, 78). With regard to sharing in the Eucharist, 'the decision as to whether the non-Catholic party of the marriage may be admitted to Eucharistic communion is to be made in keeping with the general norms existing in the matter, both for Eastern Christians and

---

[269] *Catechesis* (24 June 2015): *L'Osservatore Romano*, 25 June 2015, p. 8.

[270] *Catechesis* (5 August 2015): *L'Osservatore Romano*, 6 August 2015, p. 7.

for other Christians, taking into account the particular situation of the reception of the sacrament of matrimony by two baptized Christians. Although the spouses in a mixed marriage share the sacraments of baptism and matrimony, eucharistic sharing can only be exceptional and in each case according to the stated norms' (Pontifical Council for Promoting Christian Unity, *Directory for the Application of Principles and Norms on Ecumenism*, 25 March 1993, 159-160)".[271]

248. "Marriages involving disparity of cult represent a privileged place for interreligious dialogue in everyday life... They involve special difficulties regarding both the Christian identity of the family and the religious upbringing of the children... The number of households with married couples with disparity of cult, on the rise in mission territories, and even in countries of long Christian tradition, urgently requires providing a differentiated pastoral care according to various social and cultural contexts. In some countries where freedom of religion does not exist, the Christian spouse is obliged to convert to another religion in order to marry, and, therefore, cannot celebrate a canonical marriage involving disparity of cult or baptize the children. We must therefore reiterate the necessity that the religious freedom of all be respected".[272] "Attention needs to be given to the persons who enter such marriages, not only in the period before the wedding. Unique challenges face couples and families in which one partner is Catholic and the other is a non-believer. In such cases, bearing witness to the ability of the Gospel to immerse itself in these situations will make possible the upbringing of their children in the Christian faith".[273]

249. "Particular problems arise when persons in a complex marital situation wish to be baptized. These persons contracted a stable marriage at a time when at least one of them did not know the Christian faith. In such cases, bishops are called to exercise a pastoral discernment which is commensurate with their spiritual good".[274]

---

[271] *Relatio Finalis* 2015, 72.

[272] *Ibid.*, 73.

[273] *Ibid.*, 74.

[274] *Ibid.*, 75.

250. The Church makes her own the attitude of the Lord Jesus, who offers his boundless love to each person without exception.[275] During the Synod, we discussed the situation of families whose members include persons who experience same-sex attraction, a situation not easy either for parents or for children. We would like before all else to reaffirm that every person, regardless of sexual orientation, ought to be respected in his or her dignity and treated with consideration, while 'every sign of unjust discrimination' is to be carefully avoided,[276] particularly any form of aggression and violence. Such families should be given respectful pastoral guidance, so that those who manifest a homosexual orientation can receive the assistance they need to understand and fully carry out God's will in their lives.[277]

251. In discussing the dignity and mission of the family, the Synod Fathers observed that, "as for proposals to place unions between homosexual persons on the same level as marriage, there are absolutely no grounds for considering homosexual unions to be in any way similar or even remotely analogous to God's plan for marriage and family". It is unacceptable "that local Churches should be subjected to pressure in this matter and that international bodies should make financial aid to poor countries dependent on the introduction of laws to establish 'marriage' between persons of the same sex".[278]

252. Single-parent families often result from "the unwillingness of biological mothers or fathers to be part of a family; situations of violence, where one parent is forced to flee with the children; the death of one of the parents; the abandonment of the family by one parent, and other situations. Whatever the cause, single parents must receive encouragement and support from other families in the Christian community, and from the parish's pastoral outreach. Often these families endure other hardships,

[275] Bull *Misericordiae Vultus*, 12: AAS 107 (2015), 407.

[276] *Catechism of the Catholic Church*, 2358; cf. *Relatio Finalis* 2015, 76.

[277] *Ibid.*

[278] *Relatio Finalis* 2015, 76; cf. CONGREGATION FOR THE DOCTRINE OF THE FAITH, *Considerations Regarding Proposals to Give Legal Recognition to Unions between Homosexual Persons* (3 June 2003), 4.

such as economic difficulties, uncertain employment prospects, problems with child support and lack of housing".[279]

WHEN DEATH MAKES US FEEL ITS STING

253. At times family life is challenged by the death of a loved one. We cannot fail to offer the light of faith as a support to families going through this experience.[280] To turn our backs on a grieving family would show a lack of mercy, mean the loss of a pastoral opportunity, and close the door to other efforts at evangelization.

254. I can understand the anguish felt by those who have lost a much-loved person, a spouse with whom they have shared so much. Jesus himself was deeply moved and began to weep at the death of a friend (cf. *Jn* 11:33, 35). And how can we even begin to understand the grief of parents who have lost a child? "It is as if time stops altogether: a chasm opens to engulf both past and future", and "at times we even go so far as to lay the blame on God. How many people - I can understand them - get angry with God".[281] "Losing one's spouse is particularly difficult... From the moment of enduring a loss, some display an ability to concentrate their energies in a greater dedication to their children and grandchildren, finding in this experience of love a renewed sense of mission in raising their children.... Those who do not have relatives to spend time with and to receive affection from, should be aided by the Christian community with particular attention and availability, especially if they are poor".[282]

255. Ordinarily, the grieving process takes a fair amount of time, and when a pastor must accompany that process, he has to adapt to the demands of each of its stages. The entire process is filled with questions: about the reasons why the loved one had to die, about all the things that might have been done, about what a person experiences at the moment of death. With a sincere and patient process of prayer and interior liberation,

---

[279] *Ibid.*, 80.

[280] Cf. *ibid.*, 20.

[281] *Catechesis* (17 June 2015): *L'Osservatore Romano*, 18 June 2015, p. 8.

[282] *Relatio Finalis* 2015, 19.

peace returns. At particular times, we have to help the grieving person to realize that, after the loss of a loved one, we still have a mission to carry out, and that it does us no good to prolong the suffering, as if it were a form of tribute. Our loved ones have no need of our suffering, nor does it flatter them that we should ruin our lives. Nor is it the best expression of love to dwell on them and keep bringing up their name, because this is to be dependent on the past instead of continuing to love them now that they are elsewhere. They can no longer be physically present to us, yet for all death's power, "love is strong as death" (*Song* 8:6). Love involves an intuition that can enable us to hear without sounds and to see the unseen. This does not mean imagining our loved ones as they were, but being able to accept them changed as they now are. The risen Jesus, when his friend Mary tried to embrace him, told her not to hold on to him (cf. *Jn* 20:17), in order to lead her to a different kind of encounter.

256. It consoles us to know that those who die do not completely pass away, and faith assures us that the risen Lord will never abandon us. Thus we can "prevent death from poisoning life, from rendering vain our love, from pushing us into the darkest chasm".[283] The Bible tells us that God created us out of love and made us in such a way that our life does not end with death (cf. *Wis* 3:2-3). Saint Paul speaks to us of an encounter with Christ immediately after death: "My desire is to depart and be with Christ" (*Phil* 1:23). With Christ, after death, there awaits us "what God has prepared for those who love him" (*1 Cor* 2:9). The Preface of the Liturgy of the Dead puts it nicely: "Although the certainty of death saddens us, we are consoled by the promise of future immortality. For the life of those who believe in you, Lord, is not ended but changed". Indeed, "our loved ones are not lost in the shades of nothingness; hope assures us that they are in the good strong hands of God".[284]

257. One way of maintaining fellowship with our loved ones is to pray for them.[285] The Bible tells us that "to pray for the dead" is "holy and pious" (*2 Macc* 12:44-45). "Our prayer for them is capable not only of

---

[283] *Catechesis* (17 June 2015): *L'Osservatore Romano*, 18 June 2015, p. 8.

[284] *Ibid.*

[285] Cf. *Catechism of the Catholic Church*, 958.

helping them, but also of making their intercession for us effective".[286] The Book of Revelation portrays the martyrs interceding for those who suffer injustice on earth (cf. *Rev* 6:9-11), in solidarity with this world and its history. Some saints, before dying, consoled their loved ones by promising them that they would be near to help them. Saint Thérèse of Lisieux wished to continue doing good from heaven.[287] Saint Dominic stated that "he would be more helpful after death... more powerful in obtaining graces".[288] These are truly "bonds of love",[289] because "the union of the wayfarers with the brethren who sleep in the Lord is in no way interrupted... [but] reinforced by an exchange of spiritual goods".[290]

258. If we accept death, we can prepare ourselves for it. The way is to grow in our love for those who walk at our side, until that day when "death will be no more, mourning and crying and pain will be no more" (*Rev* 21:4). We will thus prepare ourselves to meet once more our loved ones who have died. Just as Jesus "gave back to his mother" (cf. *Lk* 7:15) her son who had died, so it will be with us. Let us not waste energy by dwelling on the distant past. The better we live on this earth, the greater the happiness we will be able to share with our loved ones in heaven. The more we are able to mature and develop in this world, the more gifts will we be able to bring to the heavenly banquet.

---

[286] *Ibid.*

[287] Cf. THÉRÈSE OF LISIEUX, *Derniers Entretiens: Le "carnet jaune" de Mère Agnès*, 17 July 1897, in *Oeuvres Complètes*, Paris, 1996, 1050. Her Carmelite sisters spoke of a promise made by Saint Thérèse that her departure from this world would be "like a shower of roses" (*ibid.*, 9 June 1897, 1013).

[288] JORDAN OF SAXONY, *Libellus de principiis Ordinis Praedicatorum*, 93: *Monumenta Historica Sancti Patris Nostri Dominici*, XVI, Rome, 1935, p. 69.

[289] Cf. *Catechism of the Catholic Church*, 957.

[290] SECOND VATICAN ECUMENICAL COUNCIL, Dogmatic Constitution on the Church *Lumen Gentium*, 49.

CHAPTER SEVEN

TOWARDS A BETTER EDUCATION OF CHILDREN

259. Parents always influence the moral development of their children, for better or for worse. It follows that they should take up this essential role and carry it out consciously, enthusiastically, reasonably and appropriately. Since the educational role of families is so important, and increasingly complex, I would like to discuss it in detail.

WHERE ARE OUR CHILDREN?

260. Families cannot help but be places of support, guidance and direction, however much they may have to rethink their methods and discover new resources. Parents need to consider what they want their children to be exposed to, and this necessarily means being concerned about who is providing their entertainment, who is entering their rooms through television and electronic devices, and with whom they are spending their free time. Only if we devote time to our children, speaking of important things with simplicity and concern, and finding healthy ways for them to spend their time, will we be able to shield them from harm. Vigilance is always necessary and neglect is never beneficial. Parents have to help prepare children and adolescents to confront the risk, for example, of aggression, abuse or drug addiction.

261. Obsession, however, is not education. We cannot control every situation that a child may experience. Here it remains true that "time is greater than space".[291] In other words, it is more important to start processes than to dominate spaces. If parents are obsessed with always knowing where their children are and controlling all their movements, they will seek only to dominate space. But this is no way to educate, strengthen and prepare their children to face challenges. What is most important is the ability lovingly to help them grow in freedom, maturity,

---

[291] Apostolic Exhortation *Evangelii Gaudium* (24 November 2013), 222: AAS 105 (2013), 1111.

overall discipline and real autonomy. Only in this way will children come to possess the wherewithal needed to fend for themselves and to act intelligently and prudently whenever they meet with difficulties. The real question, then, is not where our children are physically, or whom they are with at any given time, but rather where they are existentially, where they stand in terms of their convictions, goals, desires and dreams. The questions I would put to parents are these: "Do we seek to understand 'where' our children really are in their journey? Where is their soul, do we really know? And above all, do we want to know?".[292]

262. Were maturity merely the development of something already present in our genetic code, not much would have to be done. But prudence, good judgement and common sense are dependent not on purely quantitative growth factors, but rather on a whole series of things that come together deep within each person, or better, at the very core of our freedom. Inevitably, each child will surprise us with ideas and projects born of that freedom, which challenge us to rethink our own ideas. This is a good thing. Education includes encouraging the responsible use of freedom to face issues with good sense and intelligence. It involves forming persons who readily understand that their own lives, and the life of the community, are in their hands, and that freedom is itself a great gift.

THE ETHICAL FORMATION OF CHILDREN

263. Parents rely on schools to ensure the basic instruction of their children, but can never completely delegate the moral formation of their children to others. A person's affective and ethical development is ultimately grounded in a particular experience, namely, that his or her parents can be trusted. This means that parents, as educators, are responsible, by their affection and example, for instilling in their children trust and loving respect. When children no longer feel that, for all their faults, they are important to their parents, or that their parents are sincerely concerned about them, this causes deep hurt and many difficulties along their path to maturity. This physical or emotional absence creates greater hurt than any scolding which a child may receive for doing something wrong.

---

[292] *Catechesis* (20 May 2015): *L'Osservatore Romano*, 21 May 2015, p. 8.

264. Parents are also responsible for shaping the will of their children, fostering good habits and a natural inclination to goodness. This entails presenting certain ways of thinking and acting as desirable and worthwhile, as part of a gradual process of growth. The desire to fit into society, or the habit of foregoing an immediate pleasure for the sake of a better and more orderly life in common, is itself a value that can then inspire openness to greater values. Moral formation should always take place with active methods and a dialogue that teaches through sensitivity and by using a language children can understand. It should also take place inductively, so that children can learn for themselves the importance of certain values, principles and norms, rather than by imposing these as absolute and unquestionable truths.

265. Doing what is right means more than "judging what seems best" or knowing clearly what needs to be done, as important as this is. Often we prove inconsistent in our own convictions, however firm they may be; even when our conscience dictates a clear moral decision, other factors sometimes prove more attractive and powerful. We have to arrive at the point where the good that the intellect grasps can take root in us as a profound affective inclination, as a thirst for the good that outweighs other attractions and helps us to realize that what we consider objectively good is also good "for us" here and now. A good ethical education includes showing a person that it is in his own interest to do what is right. Today, it is less and less effective to demand something that calls for effort and sacrifice, without clearly pointing to the benefits which it can bring.

266. Good habits need to be developed. Even childhood habits can help to translate important interiorized values into sound and steady ways of acting. A person may be sociable and open to others, but if over a long period of time he has not been trained by his elders to say "Please", "Thank you", and "Sorry", his good interior disposition will not easily come to the fore. The strengthening of the will and the repetition of specific actions are the building blocks of moral conduct; without the conscious, free and valued repetition of certain patterns of good behaviour, moral education does not take place. Mere desire, or an attraction to a certain value, is not enough to instil a virtue in the absence of those properly motivated acts.

267. Freedom is something magnificent, yet it can also be dissipated and lost. Moral education has to do with cultivating freedom through ideas, incentives, practical applications, stimuli, rewards, examples, models, symbols, reflections, encouragement, dialogue and a constant rethinking of our way of doing things; all these can help develop those stable interior principles that lead us spontaneously to do good. Virtue is a conviction that has become a steadfast inner principle of operation. The virtuous life thus builds, strengthens and shapes freedom, lest we become slaves of dehumanizing and antisocial inclinations. For human dignity itself demands that each of us "act out of conscious and free choice, as moved and drawn in a personal way from within".[293]

THE VALUE OF CORRECTION AS AN INCENTIVE

268. It is also essential to help children and adolescents to realize that misbehaviour has consequences. They need to be encouraged to put themselves in other people's shoes and to acknowledge the hurt they have caused. Some punishments - those for aggressive, antisocial conduct - can partially serve this purpose. It is important to train children firmly to ask forgiveness and to repair the harm done to others. As the educational process bears fruit in the growth of personal freedom, children come to appreciate that it was good to grow up in a family and even to put up with the demands that every process of formation makes.

269. Correction is also an incentive whenever children's efforts are appreciated and acknowledged, and they sense their parents' constant, patient trust. Children who are lovingly corrected feel cared for; they perceive that they are individuals whose potential is recognized. This does not require parents to be perfect, but to be able humbly to acknowledge their own limitations and make efforts to improve. Still, one of the things children need to learn from their parents is not to get carried away by anger. A child who does something wrong must be corrected, but never treated as an enemy or an object on which to take out one's own frustrations. Adults also need to realize that some kinds of misbehaviour have to do with the frailty and limitations typical of youth. An attitude

---

[293] SECOND VATICAN ECUMENICAL COUNCIL, Pastoral Constitution on the Church in the Modern World *Gaudium et Spes*, 17.

constantly prone to punishment would be harmful and not help children to realize that some actions are more serious than others. It would lead to discouragement and resentment: "Parents, do not provoke your children" (*Eph* 6:4; cf. *Col* 3:21).

270. It is important that discipline not lead to discouragement, but be instead a stimulus to further progress. How can discipline be best interiorized? How do we ensure that discipline is a constructive limit placed on a child's actions and not a barrier standing in the way of his or her growth? A balance has to be found between two equally harmful extremes. One would be to try to make everything revolve around the child's desires; such children will grow up with a sense of their rights but not their responsibilities. The other would be to deprive the child of an awareness of his or her dignity, personal identity and rights; such children end up overwhelmed by their duties and a need to carry out other people's wishes.

PATIENT REALISM

271. Moral education entails asking of a child or a young person only those things that do not involve a disproportionate sacrifice, and demanding only a degree of effort that will not lead to resentment or coercion. Ordinarily this is done by proposing small steps that can be understood, accepted and appreciated, while including a proportionate sacrifice. Otherwise, by demanding too much, we gain nothing. Once the child is free of our authority, he or she may possibly cease to do good.

272. Ethical formation is at times frowned upon, due to experiences of neglect, disappointment, lack of affection or poor models of parenting. Ethical values are associated with negative images of parental figures or the shortcomings of adults. For this reason, adolescents should be helped to draw analogies: to appreciate that values are best embodied in a few exemplary persons, but also realized imperfectly and to different degrees in others. At the same time, since their hesitation can be tied to bad experiences, they need help in the process of inner healing and in this way to grow in the ability to understand and live in peace with others and the larger community.

273. In proposing values, we have to proceed slowly, taking into consideration the child's age and abilities, without presuming to apply rigid and inflexible methods. The valuable contributions of psychology and the educational sciences have shown that changing a child's behaviour involves a gradual process, but also that freedom needs to be channelled and stimulated, since by itself it does not ensure growth in maturity. Situated freedom, real freedom, is limited and conditioned. It is not simply the ability to choose what is good with complete spontaneity. A distinction is not always adequately drawn between "voluntary" and "free" acts. A person may clearly and willingly desire something evil, but do so as the result of an irresistible passion or a poor upbringing. In such cases, while the decision is voluntary, inasmuch as it does not run counter to the inclination of their desire, it is not free, since it is practically impossible for them not to choose that evil. We see this in the case of compulsive drug addicts. When they want a fix, they want it completely, yet they are so conditioned that at that moment no other decision is possible. Their decision is voluntary but not free. It makes no sense to "let them freely choose", since in fact they cannot choose, and exposing them to drugs only increases their addiction. They need the help of others and a process of rehabilitation.

FAMILY LIFE AS AN EDUCATIONAL SETTING

274. The family is the first school of human values, where we learn the wise use of freedom. Certain inclinations develop in childhood and become so deeply rooted that they remain throughout life, either as attractions to a particular value or a natural repugnance to certain ways of acting. Many people think and act in a certain way because they deem it to be right on the basis of what they learned, as if by osmosis, from their earliest years: "That's how I was taught". "That's what I learned to do". In the family we can also learn to be critical about certain messages sent by the various media. Sad to say, some television programmes or forms of advertising often negatively influence and undercut the values inculcated in family life.

275. In our own day, dominated by stress and rapid technological advances, one of the most important tasks of families is to provide an education in hope. This does not mean preventing children from playing

with electronic devices, but rather finding ways to help them develop their critical abilities and not to think that digital speed can apply to everything in life. Postponing desires does not mean denying them but simply deferring their fulfilment. When children or adolescents are not helped to realize that some things have to be waited for, they can become obsessed with satisfying their immediate needs and develop the vice of "wanting it all now". This is a grand illusion which does not favour freedom but weakens it. On the other hand, when we are taught to postpone some things until the right moment, we learn self-mastery and detachment from our impulses. When children realize that they have to be responsible for themselves, their self-esteem is enriched. This in turn teaches them to respect the freedom of others. Obviously this does not mean expecting children to act like adults, but neither does it mean underestimating their ability to grow in responsible freedom. In a healthy family, this learning process usually takes place through the demands made by life in common.

276. The family is the primary setting for socialization, since it is where we first learn to relate to others, to listen and share, to be patient and show respect, to help one another and live as one. The task of education is to make us sense that the world and society are also our home; it trains us how to live together in this greater home. In the family, we learn closeness, care and respect for others. We break out of our fatal self-absorption and come to realize that we are living with and alongside others who are worthy of our concern, our kindness and our affection. There is no social bond without this primary, everyday, almost microscopic aspect of living side by side, crossing paths at different times of the day, being concerned about everything that affects us, helping one another with ordinary little things. Every day the family has to come up with new ways of appreciating and acknowledging its members.

277. In the family too, we can rethink our habits of consumption and join in caring for the environment as our common home. "The family is the principal agent of an integral ecology, because it is the primary social subject which contains within it the two fundamental principles of human civilization on earth: the principle of communion and the principle

of fruitfulness".[294] In the same way, times of difficulty and trouble in the lives of family life can teach important lessons. This happens, for example, when illness strikes, since "in the face of illness, even in families, difficulties arise due to human weakness. But in general, times of illness enable family bonds to grow stronger... An education that fails to encourage sensitivity to human illness makes the heart grow cold; it makes young people 'anesthetized' to the suffering of others, incapable of facing suffering and of living the experience of limitation".[295]

278. The educational process that occurs between parents and children can be helped or hindered by the increasing sophistication of the communications and entertainment media. When well used, these media can be helpful for connecting family members who live apart from one another. Frequent contacts help to overcome difficulties.[296] Still, it is clear that these media cannot replace the need for more personal and direct dialogue, which requires physical presence or at least hearing the voice of the other person. We know that sometimes they can keep people apart rather than together, as when at dinnertime everyone is surfing on a mobile phone, or when one spouse falls asleep waiting for the other who spends hours playing with an electronic device. This is also something that families have to discuss and resolve in ways which encourage interaction without imposing unrealistic prohibitions. In any event, we cannot ignore the risks that these new forms of communication pose for children and adolescents; at times they can foster apathy and disconnection from the real world. This "technological disconnection" exposes them more easily to manipulation by those who would invade their private space with selfish interests.

279. Nor is it good for parents to be domineering. When children are made to feel that only their parents can be trusted, this hinders an adequate process of socialization and growth in affective maturity. To help expand the parental relationship to broader realities, "Christian communities are called to offer support to the educational mission of families",[297]

---

[294] *Catechesis* (30 September 2015): *L'Osservatore Romano*, 1 October 2015, p. 8.

[295] *Catechesis* (10 June 2015): *L'Osservatore Romano*, 11 June 2015, p. 8.

[296] Cf. *Relatio Finalis* 2015, 67.

[297] *Catechesis* (20 May 2015): *L'Osservatore Romano*, 21 May 2015, p. 8.

particularly through the catechesis associated with Christian initiation. To foster an integral education, we need to "renew the covenant between the family and the Christian community".[298] The Synod wanted to emphasize the importance of Catholic schools which "play a vital role in assisting parents in their duty to raise their children... Catholic schools should be encouraged in their mission to help pupils grow into mature adults who can view the world with the love of Jesus and who can understand life as a call to serve God".[299] For this reason, "the Church strongly affirms her freedom to set forth her teaching and the right of conscientious objection on the part of educators".[300]

THE NEED FOR SEX EDUCATION

280. The Second Vatican Council spoke of the need for "a positive and prudent sex education" to be imparted to children and adolescents "as they grow older", with "due weight being given to the advances in the psychological, pedogogical and didactic sciences".[301] We may well ask ourselves if our educational institutions have taken up this challenge. It is not easy to approach the issue of sex education in an age when sexuality tends to be trivialized and impoverished. It can only be seen within the broader framework of an education for love, for mutual self-giving. In such a way, the language of sexuality would not be sadly impoverished but illuminated and enriched. The sexual urge can be directed through a process of growth in self-knowledge and self-control capable of nurturing valuable capacities for joy and for loving encounter.

281. Sex education should provide information while keeping in mind that children and young people have not yet attained full maturity. The information has to come at a proper time and in a way suited to their age. It is not helpful to overwhelm them with data without also helping them to develop a critical sense in dealing with the onslaught of new ideas and suggestions, the flood of pornography and the overload of stimuli that can

---

[298] *Catechesis* (9 September 2015): *L'Osservatore Romano*, 10 September 2015, p. 8.

[299] *Relatio Finalis* 2015, 68.

[300] *Ibid.*, 58.

[301] SECOND VATICAN ECUMENICAL COUNCIL, Declaration on Christian Education *Gravissimum Educationis*, 1.

deform sexuality. Young people need to realize that they are bombarded by messages that are not beneficial for their growth towards maturity. They should be helped to recognize and to seek out positive influences, while shunning the things that cripple their capacity for love. We also have to realize that "a new and more appropriate language" is needed "in introducing children and adolescents to the topic of sexuality".[302]

282. A sexual education that fosters a healthy sense of modesty has immense value, however much some people nowadays consider modesty a relic of a bygone era. Modesty is a natural means whereby we defend our personal privacy and prevent ourselves from being turned into objects to be used. Without a sense of modesty, affection and sexuality can be reduced to an obsession with genitality and unhealthy behaviours that distort our capacity for love, and with forms of sexual violence that lead to inhuman treatment or cause hurt to others.

283. Frequently, sex education deals primarily with "protection" through the practice of "safe sex". Such expressions convey a negative attitude towards the natural procreative finality of sexuality, as if an eventual child were an enemy to be protected against. This way of thinking promotes narcissism and aggressivity in place of acceptance. It is always irresponsible to invite adolescents to toy with their bodies and their desires, as if they possessed the maturity, values, mutual commitment and goals proper to marriage. They end up being blithely encouraged to use other persons as a means of fulfilling their needs or limitations. The important thing is to teach them sensitivity to different expressions of love, mutual concern and care, loving respect and deeply meaningful communication. All of these prepare them for an integral and generous gift of self that will be expressed, following a public commitment, in the gift of their bodies. Sexual union in marriage will thus appear as a sign of an all-inclusive commitment, enriched by everything that has preceded it.

---

[302] *Relatio Finalis* 2015, 56.

284. Young people should not be deceived into confusing two levels of reality: "sexual attraction creates, for the moment, the illusion of union, yet, without love, this 'union' leaves strangers as far apart as they were before".[303] The language of the body calls for a patient apprenticeship in learning to interpret and channel desires in view of authentic self-giving. When we presume to give everything all at once, it may well be that we give nothing. It is one thing to understand how fragile and bewildered young people can be, but another thing entirely to encourage them to prolong their immaturity in the way they show love. But who speaks of these things today? Who is capable of taking young people seriously? Who helps them to prepare seriously for a great and generous love? Where sex education is concerned, much is at stake.

285. Sex education should also include respect and appreciation for differences, as a way of helping the young to overcome their self-absorption and to be open and accepting of others. Beyond the understandable difficulties which individuals may experience, the young need to be helped to accept their own body as it was created, for "thinking that we enjoy absolute power over our own bodies turns, often subtly, into thinking that we enjoy absolute power over creation... An appreciation of our body as male or female is also necessary for our own self-awareness in an encounter with others different from ourselves. In this way we can joyfully accept the specific gifts of another man or woman, the work of God the Creator, and find mutual enrichment".[304] Only by losing the fear of being different, can we be freed of self-centredness and self-absorption. Sex education should help young people to accept their own bodies and to avoid the pretension "to cancel out sexual difference because one no longer knows how to deal with it".[305]

286. Nor can we ignore the fact that the configuration of our own mode of being, whether as male or female, is not simply the result of biological or genetic factors, but of multiple elements having to do with temperament, family history, culture, experience, education, the

---

[303] ERICH FROMM, *The Art of Loving*, New York, 1956, p. 54.

[304] Encyclical Letter *Laudato Si'* (24 May 2015), 155.

[305] *Catechesis* (15 April 2015): *L'Osservatore Romano*, 16 April 2015, p. 8.

influence of friends, family members and respected persons, as well as other formative situations. It is true that we cannot separate the masculine and the feminine from God's work of creation, which is prior to all our decisions and experiences, and where biological elements exist which are impossible to ignore. But it is also true that masculinity and femininity are not rigid categories. It is possible, for example, that a husband's way of being masculine can be flexibly adapted to the wife's work schedule. Taking on domestic chores or some aspects of raising children does not make him any less masculine or imply failure, irresponsibility or cause for shame. Children have to be helped to accept as normal such healthy "exchanges" which do not diminish the dignity of the father figure. A rigid approach turns into an over-accentuation of the masculine or feminine, and does not help children and young people to appreciate the genuine reciprocity incarnate in the real conditions of matrimony. Such rigidity, in turn, can hinder the development of an individual's abilities, to the point of leading him or her to think, for example, that it is not really masculine to cultivate art or dance, or not very feminine to exercise leadership. This, thank God, has changed, but in some places deficient notions still condition the legitimate freedom and hamper the authentic development of children's specific identity and potential.

PASSING ON THE FAITH

287. Raising children calls for an orderly process of handing on the faith. This is made difficult by current lifestyles, work schedules and the complexity of today's world, where many people keep up a frenetic pace just to survive.[306] Even so, the home must continue to be the place where we learn to appreciate the meaning and beauty of the faith, to pray and to serve our neighbour. This begins with baptism, in which, as Saint Augustine said, mothers who bring their children "co-operate in the sacred birthing".[307] Thus begins the journey of growth in that new life. Faith is God's gift, received in baptism, and not our own work, yet parents are the means that God uses for it to grow and develop. Hence "it is beautiful when mothers teach their little children to blow a kiss to Jesus or to Our Lady. How

---

[306] Cf. *Relatio Finalis* 2015, 13-14.

[307] Augustine, *De sancta virginitate* 7,7: PL 40, 400.

much love there is in that! At that moment the child's heart becomes a place of prayer".[308] Handing on the faith presumes that parents themselves genuinely trust God, seek him and sense their need for him, for only in this way does "one generation laud your works to another, and declare your mighty acts" (*Ps* 144:4) and "fathers make known to children your faithfulness" (*Is* 38:19). This means that we need to ask God to act in their hearts, in places where we ourselves cannot reach. A mustard seed, small as it is, becomes a great tree (cf. *Mt* 13:31-32); this teaches us to see the disproportion between our actions and their effects. We know that we do not own the gift, but that its care is entrusted to us. Yet our creative commitment is itself an offering which enables us to co-operate with God's plan. For this reason, "couples and parents should be properly appreciated as active agents in catechesis… Family catechesis is of great assistance as an effective method in training young parents to be aware of their mission as the evangelizers of their own family".[309]

288. Education in the faith has to adapt to each child, since older resources and recipes do not always work. Children need symbols, actions and stories. Since adolescents usually have issues with authority and rules, it is best to encourage their own experience of faith and to provide them with attractive testimonies that win them over by their sheer beauty. Parents desirous of nurturing the faith of their children are sensitive to their patterns of growth, for they know that spiritual experience is not imposed but freely proposed.
It is essential that children actually see that, for their parents, prayer is something truly important. Hence moments of family prayer and acts of devotion can be more powerful for evangelization than any catechism class or sermon. Here I would like to express my particular gratitude to all those mothers who continue to pray, like Saint Monica, for their children who have strayed from Christ.

289. The work of handing on the faith to children, in the sense of facilitating its expression and growth, helps the whole family in its evangelizing mission. It naturally begins to spread the faith to all around them, even

---

[308] *Catechesis* (26 August 2015): *L'Osservatore Romano*, 27 August 2015, p. 8.
[309] *Relatio Finalis* 2015, 89.

outside of the family circle. Children who grew up in missionary families often become missionaries themselves; growing up in warm and friendly families, they learn to relate to the world in this way, without giving up their faith or their convictions. We know that Jesus himself ate and drank with sinners (cf. *Mk* 2:16; *Mt* 11:19), conversed with a Samaritan woman (cf. *Jn* 4:7-26), received Nicodemus by night (cf. *Jn* 3:1-21), allowed his feet to be anointed by a prostitute (cf. *Lk* 7:36-50) and did not hesitate to lay his hands on those who were sick (cf. *Mk* 1:40-45; 7:33). The same was true of his apostles, who did not look down on others, or cluster together in small and elite groups, cut off from the life of their people. Although the authorities harassed them, they nonetheless enjoyed the favour "of all the people" (*Acts* 2:47; cf. 4:21, 33; 5:13).

290. "The family is thus an agent of pastoral activity through its explicit proclamation of the Gospel and its legacy of varied forms of witness, namely solidarity with the poor, openness to a diversity of people, the protection of creation, moral and material solidarity with other families, including those most in need, commitment to the promotion of the common good and the transformation of unjust social structures, beginning in the territory in which the family lives, through the practice of the corporal and spiritual works of mercy".[310] All this is an expression of our profound Christian belief in the love of the Father who guides and sustains us, a love manifested in the total self-gift of Jesus Christ, who even now lives in our midst and enables us to face together the storms of life at every stage. In all families the Good News needs to resound, in good times and in bad, as a source of light along the way. All of us should be able to say, thanks to the experience of our life in the family: "We come to believe in the love that God has for us" (*1 Jn* 4:16). Only on the basis of this experience will the Church's pastoral care for families enable them to be both domestic churches and a leaven of evangelization in society.

---

[310] *Ibid.*, 93.

CHAPTER EIGHT

ACCOMPANYING, DISCERNING AND INTEGRATING WEAKNESS

291. The Synod Fathers stated that, although the Church realizes that any breach of the marriage bond "is against the will of God", she is also "conscious of the frailty of many of her children".[311] Illumined by the gaze of Jesus Christ, "she turns with love to those who participate in her life in an incomplete manner, recognizing that the grace of God works also in their lives by giving them the courage to do good, to care for one another in love and to be of service to the community in which they live and work".[312] This approach is also confirmed by our celebration of this Jubilee Year devoted to mercy. Although she constantly holds up the call to perfection and asks for a fuller response to God, "the Church must accompany with attention and care the weakest of her children, who show signs of a wounded and troubled love, by restoring in them hope and confidence, like the beacon of a lighthouse in a port or a torch carried among the people to enlighten those who have lost their way or who are in the midst of a storm".[313] Let us not forget that the Church's task is often like that of a field hospital.

292. Christian marriage, as a reflection of the union between Christ and his Church, is fully realized in the union between a man and a woman who give themselves to each other in a free, faithful and exclusive love, who belong to each other until death and are open to the transmission of life, and are consecrated by the sacrament, which grants them the grace to become a domestic church and a leaven of new life for society. Some forms of union radically contradict this ideal, while others realize it in at least a partial and analogous way. The Synod Fathers stated that the Church does not disregard the constructive elements in those situations which do not yet or no longer correspond to her teaching on marriage.[314]

---

[311] *Relatio Synodi* 2014, 24.

[312] *Ibid*. 25.

[313] *Ibid*. 28.

[314] Cf. *ibid*., 41, 43; *Relatio Finalis* 2015, 70.

GRADUALNESS IN PASTORAL CARE

293. The Fathers also considered the specific situation of a merely civil marriage or, with due distinction, even simple cohabitation, noting that "when such unions attain a particular stability, legally recognized, are characterized by deep affection and responsibility for their offspring, and demonstrate an ability to overcome trials, they can provide occasions for pastoral care with a view to the eventual celebration of the sacrament of marriage".[315] On the other hand, it is a source of concern that many young people today distrust marriage and live together, putting off indefinitely the commitment of marriage, while yet others break a commitment already made and immediately assume a new one. "As members of the Church, they too need pastoral care that is merciful and helpful".[316] For the Church's pastors are not only responsible for promoting Christian marriage, but also the "pastoral discernment of the situations of a great many who no longer live this reality. Entering into pastoral dialogue with these persons is needed to distinguish elements in their lives that can lead to a greater openness to the Gospel of marriage in its fulness".[317] In this pastoral discernment, there is a need "to identify elements that can foster evangelization and human and spiritual growth".[318]

294. "The choice of a civil marriage or, in many cases, of simple cohabitation, is often not motivated by prejudice or resistance to a sacramental union, but by cultural or contingent situations".[319] In such cases, respect also can be shown for those signs of love which in some way reflect God's own love.[320] We know that there is "a continual increase in the number of those who, after having lived together for a long period, request the celebration of marriage in Church. Simply to live together is often a choice based on a general attitude opposed to anything institutional or definitive; it can also be done while awaiting more security in life (a steady job and steady income). In some countries, de facto unions are very

---

[315] *Ibid.*, 27.

[316] *Ibid.*, 26.

[317] *Ibid.*, 41.

[318] *Ibid.*

[319] *Relatio Finalis* 2015, 71.

[320] Cf. *ibid.*

numerous, not only because of a rejection of values concerning the family and matrimony, but primarily because celebrating a marriage is considered too expensive in the social circumstances. As a result, material poverty drives people into de facto unions".[321] Whatever the case, "all these situations require a constructive response seeking to transform them into opportunities that can lead to the full reality of marriage and family in conformity with the Gospel. These couples need to be welcomed and guided patiently and discreetly".[322] That is how Jesus treated the Samaritan woman (cf. *Jn* 4:1-26): he addressed her desire for true love, in order to free her from the darkness in her life and to bring her to the full joy of the Gospel.

295. Along these lines, Saint John Paul II proposed the so-called "law of gradualness" in the knowledge that the human being "knows, loves and accomplishes moral good by different stages of growth".[323] This is not a "gradualness of law" but rather a gradualness in the prudential exercise of free acts on the part of subjects who are not in a position to understand, appreciate, or fully carry out the objective demands of the law. For the law is itself a gift of God which points out the way, a gift for everyone without exception; it can be followed with the help of grace, even though each human being "advances gradually with the progressive integration of the gifts of God and the demands of God's definitive and absolute love in his or her entire personal and social life".[324]

THE DISCERNMENT OF "IRREGULAR" SITUATIONS [325]

296. The Synod addressed various situations of weakness or imperfection. Here I would like to reiterate something I sought to make clear to the whole Church, lest we take the wrong path: "There are two ways of thinking which recur throughout the Church's history: casting off and reinstating. The Church's way, from the time of the Council of Jerusalem,

---

[321] *Relatio Synodi* 2014, 42.

[322] *Ibid.*, 43.

[323] Apostolic Exhortation *Familiaris Consortio* (22 November 1981), 34: AAS 74 (1982), 123.

[324] Ibid., 9: AAS 74 (1982), 90.

[325] Cf. *Catechesis* (24 June 2015): *L'Osservatore Romano*, 25 June 2015, p. 8.

has always been the way of Jesus, the way of mercy and reinstatement... The way of the Church is not to condemn anyone for ever; it is to pour out the balm of God's mercy on all those who ask for it with a sincere heart... For true charity is always unmerited, unconditional and gratuitous".[326] Consequently, there is a need "to avoid judgements which do not take into account the complexity of various situations" and "to be attentive, by necessity, to how people experience distress because of their condition".[327]

297. It is a matter of reaching out to everyone, of needing to help each person find his or her proper way of participating in the ecclesial community and thus to experience being touched by an "unmerited, unconditional and gratuitous" mercy. No one can be condemned forever, because that is not the logic of the Gospel! Here I am not speaking only of the divorced and remarried, but of everyone, in whatever situation they find themselves. Naturally, if someone flaunts an objective sin as if it were part of the Christian ideal, or wants to impose something other than what the Church teaches, he or she can in no way presume to teach or preach to others; this is a case of something which separates from the community (cf. *Mt* 18:17). Such a person needs to listen once more to the Gospel message and its call to conversion. Yet even for that person there can be some way of taking part in the life of community, whether in social service, prayer meetings or another way that his or her own initiative, together with the discernment of the parish priest, may suggest. As for the way of dealing with different "irregular" situations, the Synod Fathers reached a general consensus, which I support: "In considering a pastoral approach towards people who have contracted a civil marriage, who are divorced and remarried, or simply living together, the Church has the responsibility of helping them understand the divine pedagogy of grace in their lives and offering them assistance so they can reach the fulness of God's plan for them",[328] something which is always possible by the power of the Holy Spirit.

---

[326] *Homily at Mass Celebrated with the New Cardinals* (15 February 2015): AAS 107 (2015), 257.

[327] *Relatio Finalis* 2015, 51.

[328] *Relatio Synodi* 2014, 25.

298. The divorced who have entered a new union, for example, can find themselves in a variety of situations, which should not be pigeonholed or fitted into overly rigid classifications leaving no room for a suitable personal and pastoral discernment. One thing is a second union consolidated over time, with new children, proven fidelity, generous self giving, Christian commitment, a consciousness of its irregularity and of the great difficulty of going back without feeling in conscience that one would fall into new sins. The Church acknowledges situations "where, for serious reasons, such as the children's upbringing, a man and woman cannot satisfy the obligation to separate".[329] There are also the cases of those who made every effort to save their first marriage and were unjustly abandoned, or of "those who have entered into a second union for the sake of the children's upbringing, and are sometimes subjectively certain in conscience that their previous and irreparably broken marriage had never been valid".[330] Another thing is a new union arising from a recent divorce, with all the suffering and confusion which this entails for children and entire families, or the case of someone who has consistently failed in his obligations to the family. It must remain clear that this is not the ideal which the Gospel proposes for marriage and the family. The Synod Fathers stated that the discernment of pastors must always take place "by adequately distinguishing",[331] with an approach which "carefully discerns situations".[332] We know that no "easy recipes" exist.[333]

299. I am in agreement with the many Synod Fathers who observed that "the baptized who are divorced and civilly remarried need to be more fully integrated into Christian communities in the variety of ways possible,

---

[329] JOHN PAUL II, Apostolic Exhortation *Familiaris Consortio* (22 November 1981), 84: AAS 74 (1982), 186. In such situations, many people, knowing and accepting the possibility of living "as brothers and sisters" which the Church offers them, point out that if certain expressions of intimacy are lacking, "it often happens that faithfulness is endangered and the good of the children suffers" (SECOND VATICAN ECUMENICAL COUNCIL, Pastoral Constitution on the Church in the Modern World *Gaudium et Spes*, 51).

[330] *Ibid.*

[331] *Relatio Synodi* 2014, 26.

[332] *Ibid.*, 45.

[333] BENEDICT XVI, *Address to the Seventh World Meeting of Families* in Milan (2 June 2012), Response n. 5: *Insegnamenti* VIII/1 (2012), 691.

while avoiding any occasion of scandal. The logic of integration is the key to their pastoral care, a care which would allow them not only to realize that they belong to the Church as the body of Christ, but also to know that they can have a joyful and fruitful experience in it. They are baptized; they are brothers and sisters; the Holy Spirit pours into their hearts gifts and talents for the good of all. Their participation can be expressed in different ecclesial services, which necessarily requires discerning which of the various forms of exclusion currently practised in the liturgical, pastoral, educational and institutional framework, can be surmounted. Such persons need to feel not as excommunicated members of the Church, but instead as living members, able to live and grow in the Church and experience her as a mother who welcomes them always, who takes care of them with affection and encourages them along the path of life and the Gospel. This integration is also needed in the care and Christian upbringing of their children, who ought to be considered most important".[334]

300. If we consider the immense variety of concrete situations such as those I have mentioned, it is understandable that neither the Synod nor this Exhortation could be expected to provide a new set of general rules, canonical in nature and applicable to all cases. What is possible is simply a renewed encouragement to undertake a responsible personal and pastoral discernment of particular cases, one which would recognize that, since "the degree of responsibility is not equal in all cases",[335] the consequences or effects of a rule need not necessarily always be the same.[336] Priests have the duty to "accompany [the divorced and remarried] in helping them to understand their situation according to the teaching of the Church and the guidelines of the bishop. Useful in this process is an examination of conscience through moments of reflection and repentance. The divorced and remarried should ask themselves: how did they act towards their children when the conjugal union entered into crisis; whether or not they made attempts at reconciliation; what has become of the abandoned party;

---

[334] *Relatio Finalis* 2015, 84.

[335] *Ibid.*, 51.

[336] This is also the case with regard to sacramental discipline, since discernment can recognize that in a particular situation no grave fault exists. In such cases, what is found in another document applies: cf. *Evangelii Gaudium* (24 November 2013), 44 and 47: AAS 105 (2013), 1038-1040.

what consequences the new relationship has on the rest of the family and the community of the faithful; and what example is being set for young people who are preparing for marriage. A sincere reflection can strengthen trust in the mercy of God which is not denied anyone".[337] What we are speaking of is a process of accompaniment and discernment which "guides the faithful to an awareness of their situation before God. Conversation with the priest, in the internal forum, contributes to the formation of a correct judgement on what hinders the possibility of a fuller participation in the life of the Church and on what steps can foster it and make it grow. Given that gradualness is not in the law itself (cf. *Familiaris Consortio*, 34), this discernment can never prescind from the Gospel demands of truth and charity, as proposed by the Church. For this discernment to happen, the following conditions must necessarily be present: humility, discretion and love for the Church and her teaching, in a sincere search for God's will and a desire to make a more perfect response to it".[338] These attitudes are essential for avoiding the grave danger of misunderstandings, such as the notion that any priest can quickly grant "exceptions", or that some people can obtain sacramental privileges in exchange for favours. When a responsible and tactful person, who does not presume to put his or her own desires ahead of the common good of the Church, meets with a pastor capable of acknowledging the seriousness of the matter before him, there can be no risk that a specific discernment may lead people to think that the Church maintains a double standard.

MITIGATING FACTORS IN PASTORAL DISCERNMENT

301. For an adequate understanding of the possibility and need of special discernment in certain "irregular" situations, one thing must always be taken into account, lest anyone think that the demands of the Gospel are in any way being compromised. The Church possesses a solid body of reflection concerning mitigating factors and situations. Hence it can no longer simply be said that all those in any "irregular" situation are living in a state of mortal sin and are deprived of sanctifying grace. More is involved here than mere ignorance of the rule. A subject may know full well the rule,

---

[337] *Relatio Finalis* 2015, 85.

[338] *Ibid.*, 86.

yet have great difficulty in understanding "its inherent values",[339] or be in a concrete situation which does not allow him or her to act differently and decide otherwise without further sin. As the Synod Fathers put it, "factors may exist which limit the ability to make a decision".[340] Saint Thomas Aquinas himself recognized that someone may possess grace and charity, yet not be able to exercise any one of the virtues well;[341] in other words, although someone may possess all the infused moral virtues, he does not clearly manifest the existence of one of them, because the outward practice of that virtue is rendered difficult: "Certain saints are said not to possess certain virtues, in so far as they experience difficulty in the acts of those virtues, even though they have the habits of all the virtues".[342]

302. The *Catechism of the Catholic Church* clearly mentions these factors: "imputability and responsibility for an action can be diminished or even nullified by ignorance, inadvertence, duress, fear, habit, inordinate attachments, and other psychological or social factors".[343] In another paragraph, the *Catechism* refers once again to circumstances which mitigate moral responsibility, and mentions at length "affective immaturity, force of acquired habit, conditions of anxiety or other psychological or social factors that lessen or even extenuate moral culpability".[344] For this reason, a negative judgement about an objective situation does not imply a judgement about the imputability or culpability of the person involved.[345] On the basis of these convictions, I consider very fitting what many Synod Fathers wanted to affirm: "Under certain circumstances people find it

---

[339] JOHN PAUL II, Apostolic Exhortation *Familiaris Consortio* (22 November 1981), 33: AAS 74 (1982), 121.

[340] *Relatio Finalis* 2015, 51.

[341] Cf. *Summa Theologiae* I-II, q. 65, art. 3 ad 2; *De Malo*, q. 2, art. 2.

[342] *Ibid.*, ad 3.

[343] No. 1735.

[344] *Ibid.*, 2352; CONGREGATION FOR THE DOCTRINE OF THE FAITH, Declaration on Euthanasia *Iura et Bona* (5 May 1980), II: AAS 72 (1980), 546; John Paul II, in his critique of the category of "fundamental option", recognized that "doubtless there can occur situations which are very complex and obscure from a psychological viewpoint, and which have an influence on the sinner's subjective culpability" (Apostolic Exhortation *Reconciliatio et Paenitentia* [2 December 1984], 17: AAS 77 [1985], 223).

[345] Cf. PONTIFICAL COUNCIL FOR LEGISLATIVE TEXTS, *Declaration Concerning the Admission to Holy Communion of Faithful Who are Divorced and Remarried* (24 June 2000), 2.

very difficult to act differently. Therefore, while upholding a general rule, it is necessary to recognize that responsibility with respect to certain actions or decisions is not the same in all cases. Pastoral discernment, while taking into account a person's properly formed conscience, must take responsibility for these situations. Even the consequences of actions taken are not necessarily the same in all cases".[346]

303. Recognizing the influence of such concrete factors, we can add that individual conscience needs to be better incorporated into the Church's praxis in certain situations which do not objectively embody our understanding of marriage. Naturally, every effort should be made to encourage the development of an enlightened conscience, formed and guided by the responsible and serious discernment of one's pastor, and to encourage an ever greater trust in God's grace. Yet conscience can do more than recognize that a given situation does not correspond objectively to the overall demands of the Gospel. It can also recognize with sincerity and honesty what for now is the most generous response which can be given to God, and come to see with a certain moral security that it is what God himself is asking amid the concrete complexity of one's limits, while yet not fully the objective ideal. In any event, let us recall that this discernment is dynamic; it must remain ever open to new stages of growth and to new decisions which can enable the ideal to be more fully realized.

RULES AND DISCERNMENT

304. It is reductive simply to consider whether or not an individual's actions correspond to a general law or rule, because that is not enough to discern and ensure full fidelity to God in the concrete life of a human being. I earnestly ask that we always recall a teaching of Saint Thomas Aquinas and learn to incorporate it in our pastoral discernment: "Although there is necessity in the general principles, the more we descend to matters of detail, the more frequently we encounter defects... In matters of action, truth or practical rectitude is not the same for all, as to matters of detail, but only as to the general principles; and where there is the same rectitude in matters of detail, it is not equally known to all... The principle will be

---

[346] *Relatio Finalis* 2015, 85.

found to fail, according as we descend further into detail".[347] It is true that general rules set forth a good which can never be disregarded or neglected, but in their formulation they cannot provide absolutely for all particular situations. At the same time, it must be said that, precisely for that reason, what is part of a practical discernment in particular circumstances cannot be elevated to the level of a rule. That would not only lead to an intolerable casuistry, but would endanger the very values which must be preserved with special care.[348]

305. For this reason, a pastor cannot feel that it is enough simply to apply moral laws to those living in "irregular" situations, as if they were stones to throw at people's lives. This would bespeak the closed heart of one used to hiding behind the Church's teachings, "sitting on the chair of Moses and judging at times with superiority and superficiality difficult cases and wounded families".[349] Along these same lines, the International Theological Commission has noted that "natural law could not be presented as an already established set of rules that impose themselves *a priori* on the moral subject; rather, it is a source of objective inspiration for the deeply personal process of making decisions".[350] Because of forms of conditioning and mitigating factors, it is possible that in an objective situation of sin - which may not be subjectively culpable, or fully such - a person can be living in God's grace, can love and can also grow in the life of grace and charity, while receiving the Church's help to this end.[351] Discernment must help to find possible ways of responding to

---

[347] *Summa Theologiae*, I-II, q. 94, art. 4.

[348] In another text, referring to the general knowledge of the rule and the particular knowledge of practical discernment, Saint Thomas states that "if only one of the two is present, it is preferable that it be the knowledge of the particular reality, which is closer to the act": *Sententia libri Ethicorum*, VI, 6 (ed. Leonina, t. XLVII, 354.)

[349] *Address for the Conclusion of the Fourteenth Ordinary General Assembly of the Synod of Bishops* (24 October 2015): *L'Osservatore Romano*, 26-27 October 2015, p. 13.

[350] INTERNATIONAL THEOLOGICAL COMMISSION, *In Search of a Universal Ethic: A New Look at Natural Law* (2009), 59.

[351] In certain cases, this can include the help of the sacraments. Hence, "I want to remind priests that the confessional must not be a torture chamber, but rather an encounter with the Lord's mercy" (Apostolic Exhortation *Evangelii Gaudium* [24 November 2013], 44: AAS 105 [2013], 1038). I would also point out that the Eucharist "is not a prize for the perfect, but a powerful medicine and nourishment for the weak" (*ibid.*, 47: 1039).

God and growing in the midst of limits. By thinking that everything is black and white, we sometimes close off the way of grace and of growth, and discourage paths of sanctification which give glory to God. Let us remember that "a small step, in the midst of great human limitations, can be more pleasing to God than a life which appears outwardly in order, but moves through the day without confronting great difficulties".[352] The practical pastoral care of ministers and of communities must not fail to embrace this reality.

306. In every situation, when dealing with those who have difficulties in living God's law to the full, the invitation to pursue the *via caritatis* must be clearly heard. Fraternal charity is the first law of Christians (cf. *Jn* 15:12; *Gal* 5:14). Let us not forget the reassuring words of Scripture: "Maintain constant love for one another, for love covers a multitude of sins" (*1 Pet* 4:8); "Atone for your sins with righteousness, and your iniquities with mercy to the oppressed, so that your prosperity may be prolonged" (*Dan* 4:24[27]); "As water extinguishes a blazing fire, so almsgiving atones for sins" (*Sir* 3:30). This is also what Saint Augustine teaches: "Just as, at the threat of a fire, we would run for water to extinguish it... so too, if the flame of sin rises from our chaff and we are troubled, if the chance to perform a work of mercy is offered us, let us rejoice in it, as if it were a fountain offered us to extinguish the blaze".[353]

THE LOGIC OF PASTORAL MERCY

307. In order to avoid all misunderstanding, I would point out that in no way must the Church desist from proposing the full ideal of marriage, God's plan in all its grandeur: "Young people who are baptized should be encouraged to understand that the sacrament of marriage can enrich their prospects of love and that they can be sustained by the grace of Christ in the sacrament and by the possibility of participating fully in the life of the Church".[354] A lukewarm attitude, any kind of relativism, or an

---

[352] Apostolic Exhortation *Evangelii Gaudium* (24 November 2013), 44: AAS 105 (2013), 1038-1039.

[353] *De Catechizandis Rudibus*, I, 14, 22: PL 40, 327; cf. Apostolic Exhortation *Evangelii Gaudium* (24 November 2013), 194: AAS 105 (2013), 1101.

[354] *Relatio Synodi* 2014, 26.

undue reticence in proposing that ideal, would be a lack of fidelity to the Gospel and also of love on the part of the Church for young people themselves. To show understanding in the face of exceptional situations never implies dimming the light of the fuller ideal, or proposing less than what Jesus offers to the human being. Today, more important than the pastoral care of failures is the pastoral effort to strengthen marriages and thus to prevent their breakdown.

308. At the same time, from our awareness of the weight of mitigating circumstances - psychological, historical and even biological - it follows that "without detracting from the evangelical ideal, there is a need to accompany with mercy and patience the eventual stages of personal growth as these progressively appear", making room for "the Lord's mercy, which spurs us on to do our best".[355] I understand those who prefer a more rigorous pastoral care which leaves no room for confusion. But I sincerely believe that Jesus wants a Church attentive to the goodness which the Holy Spirit sows in the midst of human weakness, a Mother who, while clearly expressing her objective teaching, "always does what good she can, even if in the process, her shoes get soiled by the mud of the street".[356] The Church's pastors, in proposing to the faithful the full ideal of the Gospel and the Church's teaching, must also help them to treat the weak with compassion, avoiding aggravation or unduly harsh or hasty judgements. The Gospel itself tells us not to judge or condemn (cf. *Mt* 7:1; *Lk* 6:37). Jesus "expects us to stop looking for those personal or communal niches which shelter us from the maelstrom of human misfortune, and instead to enter into the reality of other people's lives and to know the power of tenderness. Whenever we do so, our lives become wonderfully complicated".[357]

309. It is providential that these reflections take place in the context of a Holy Year devoted to mercy, because also in the variety of situations affecting families "the Church is commissioned to proclaim the mercy

---

[355] Apostolic Exhortation *Evangelii Gaudium* (24 November 2013) 44: AAS 105 (2013), 1038.

[356] *Ibid.*, 45.

[357] *Ibid.*, 270.

of God, the beating heart of the Gospel, which in its own way must penetrate the mind and heart of every person. The Bride of Christ must pattern her behaviour after the Son of God who goes out to everyone without exception".[358] She knows that Jesus himself is the shepherd of the hundred, not just of the ninety-nine. He loves them all. On the basis of this realization, it will become possible for "the balm of mercy to reach everyone, believers and those far away, as a sign that the kingdom of God is already present in our midst".[359]

310. We cannot forget that "mercy is not only the working of the Father; it becomes a criterion for knowing who his true children are. In a word, we are called to show mercy because mercy was first shown to us".[360] This is not sheer romanticism or a lukewarm response to God's love, which always seeks what is best for us, for "mercy is the very foundation of the Church's life. All of her pastoral activity should be caught up in the tenderness which she shows to believers; nothing in her preaching and her witness to the world can be lacking in mercy".[361] It is true that at times "we act as arbiters of grace rather than its facilitators. But the Church is not a tollhouse; it is the house of the Father, where there is a place for everyone, with all their problems".[362]

311. The teaching of moral theology should not fail to incorporate these considerations, for although it is quite true that concern must be shown for the integrity of the Church's moral teaching, special care should always be shown to emphasize and encourage the highest and most central values of the Gospel,[363] particularly the primacy of charity as a response to the completely gratuitous offer of God's love. At times we find it hard to make room for God's unconditional love in our

---

[358] Bull *Misericordiae Vultus* (11 April 2015), 12: AAS 107 (2015): 407.

[359] *Ibid.*, 5: 402.

[360] *Ibid.*, 9: 405.

[361] *Ibid.*, 10: 406.

[362] Apostolic Exhortation *Evangelii Gaudium* (24 November 2013), 47: AAS 105 (2013), 1040.

[363] Cf. *ibid.*, 36-37: AAS 105 (2013), 1035.

pastoral activity.[364] We put so many conditions on mercy that we empty it of its concrete meaning and real significance. That is the worst way of watering down the Gospel. It is true, for example, that mercy does not exclude justice and truth, but first and foremost we have to say that mercy is the fulness of justice and the most radiant manifestation of God's truth. For this reason, we should always consider "inadequate any theological conception which in the end puts in doubt the omnipotence of God and, especially, his mercy".[365]

312. This offers us a framework and a setting which help us avoid a cold bureaucratic morality in dealing with more sensitive issues. Instead, it sets us in the context of a pastoral discernment filled with merciful love, which is ever ready to understand, forgive, accompany, hope and above all integrate. That is the mindset which should prevail in the Church and lead us to "open our hearts to those living on the outermost fringes of society".[366] I encourage the faithful who find themselves in complicated situations to speak confidently with their pastors or with other lay people whose lives are committed to the Lord. They may not always encounter in them a confirmation of their own ideas or desires, but they will surely receive some light to help them better understand their situation and discover a path to personal growth. I also encourage the Church's pastors to listen to them with sensitivity and serenity, with a sincere desire to understand their plight and their point of view, in order to help them live better lives and to recognize their proper place in the Church.

---

[364] Perhaps out of a certain scrupulosity, concealed beneath a zeal for fidelity to the truth, some priests demand of penitents a purpose of amendment so lacking in nuance that it causes mercy to be obscured by the pursuit of a supposedly pure justice. For this reason, it is helpful to recall the teaching of Saint John Paul II, who stated that the possibility of a new fall "should not prejudice the authenticity of the resolution" (*Letter to Cardinal William W. Baum on the occasion of the Course on the Internal Forum organized by the Apostolic Penitentiary* [22 March 1996], 5: *Insegnamenti* XIX/1 [1996], 589).

[365] INTERNATIONAL THEOLOGICAL COMMISSION, *The Hope of Salvation for Infants Who Die Without Being Baptized* (19 April 2007), 2.

[366] Bull *Misericordiae Vultus* (11 April 2015), 15: AAS 107 (2015), 409.

CHAPTER NINE

THE SPIRITUALITY OF MARRIAGE AND THE FAMILY

313. Charity takes on different hues, depending on the state of life to which we have been called. Several decades ago, in speaking of the lay apostolate, the Second Vatican Council emphasized the spirituality born of family life. The Council stated that lay spirituality "will take its particular character from the circumstances of… married and family life",[367] and that "family cares should not be foreign" to that spirituality.[368] It is worth pausing to describe certain basic characteristics of this specific spirituality that unfolds in family life and its relationships.

A SPIRITUALITY OF SUPERNATURAL COMMUNION

314. We have always spoken of how God dwells in the hearts of those living in his grace. Today we can add that the Trinity is present in the temple of marital communion. Just as God dwells in the praises of his people (cf. *Ps* 22:3), so he dwells deep within the marital love that gives him glory.

315. The Lord's presence dwells in real and concrete families, with all their daily troubles and struggles, joys and hopes. Living in a family makes it hard for us to feign or lie; we cannot hide behind a mask. If that authenticity is inspired by love, then the Lord reigns there, with his joy and his peace. The spirituality of family love is made up of thousands of small but real gestures. In that variety of gifts and encounters which deepen communion, God has his dwelling place. This mutual concern "brings together the human and the divine",[369] for it is filled with the love of God. In the end, marital spirituality is a spirituality of the bond, in which divine love dwells.

---

[367] Decree on the Apostolate of the Laity *Apostolicam Actuositatem*, 4.

[368] Cf. *ibid.*

[369] SECOND VATICAN ECUMENICAL COUNCIL, Pastoral Constitution on the Church in the Modern World *Gaudium et Spes*, 49.

316. A positive experience of family communion is a true path to daily sanctification and mystical growth, a means for deeper union with God. The fraternal and communal demands of family life are an incentive to growth in openness of heart and thus to an ever fuller encounter with the Lord. The word of God tells us that "the one who hates his brother is in the darkness, and walks in the darkness" (*1 Jn* 2:11); such a person "abides in death" (*1 Jn* 3:14) and "does not know God" (*1 Jn* 4:8). My predecessor Benedict XVI pointed out that "closing our eyes to our neighbour also blinds us to God",[370] and that, in the end, love is the only light which can "constantly illuminate a world grown dim".[371] If only we "love one another, God abides in us and his love is perfected in us" (*1 Jn* 4:12). Since "the human person has an inherent social dimension",[372] and "the first and basic expression of that social dimension of the person is the married couple and the family",[373] spirituality becomes incarnate in the communion of the family. Hence, those who have deep spiritual aspirations should not feel that the family detracts from their growth in the life of the Spirit, but rather see it as a path which the Lord is using to lead them to the heights of mystical union.

GATHERED IN PRAYER IN THE LIGHT OF EASTER

317. If a family is centred on Christ, he will unify and illumine its entire life. Moments of pain and difficulty will be experienced in union with the Lord's cross, and his closeness will make it possible to surmount them. In the darkest hours of a family's life, union with Jesus in his abandonment can help avoid a breakup. Gradually, "with the grace of the Holy Spirit, [the spouses] grow in holiness through married life, also by sharing in the mystery of Christ's cross, which transforms difficulties and sufferings into an offering of love".[374] Moreover, moments of joy, relaxation, celebration, and even sexuality can be experienced as a sharing in the full life of the resurrection. Married couples shape with different daily

---

[370] Encyclical Letter *Deus Caritas Est* (25 December 2015), 16: AAS 98 (2006), 230.

[371] *Ibid.*, 39: AAS 98 (2006), 250.

[372] JOHN PAUL II, Post-Synodal Apostolic Exhortation *Christifideles Laici* (30 December 1988), 40: AAS 81 (1989), 468.

[373] *Ibid.*

[374] *Relatio Finalis* 2015, 87.

gestures a "God-enlightened space in which to experience the hidden presence of the risen Lord".[375]

318. Family prayer is a special way of expressing and strengthening this paschal faith.[376] A few minutes can be found each day to come together before the living God, to tell him our worries, to ask for the needs of our family, to pray for someone experiencing difficulty, to ask for help in showing love, to give thanks for life and for its blessings, and to ask Our Lady to protect us beneath her maternal mantle. With a few simple words, this moment of prayer can do immense good for our families. The various expressions of popular piety are a treasure of spirituality for many families. The family's communal journey of prayer culminates by sharing together in the Eucharist, especially in the context of the Sunday rest. Jesus knocks on the door of families, to share with them the Eucharistic supper (cf. *Rev* 3:20). There, spouses can always seal anew the paschal covenant which united them and which ought to reflect the covenant which God sealed with mankind in the cross.[377] The Eucharist is the sacrament of the new covenant, where Christ's redemptive work is carried out (cf. *Lk* 22:20). The close bond between married life and the Eucharist thus becomes all the more clear.[378] For the food of the Eucharist offers the spouses the strength and incentive needed to live the marriage covenant each day as a "domestic church".[379]

A SPIRITUALITY OF EXCLUSIVE AND FREE LOVE

319. Marriage is also the experience of belonging completely to another person. Spouses accept the challenge and aspiration of supporting one another, growing old together, and in this way reflecting God's own

---

[375] JOHN PAUL II, Post-Synodal Apostolic Exhortation *Vita Consecrata* (25 March 1996), 42: AAS 88 (1996), 416.

[376] Cf. *Relatio Finalis* 2015, 87.

[377] Cf. JOHN PAUL II, Apostolic Exhortation *Familiaris Consortio* (22 November 1981), 57: AAS 74 (1982), 150.

[378] Nor should we forget that God's covenant with his people is expressed as an espousal (cf. *Ez* 16:8, 60; *Is* 62:5; *Hos* 2:21-22), and that the new covenant is also presented as a betrothal (cf. *Rev* 19:7; 21:2; *Eph* 5:25).

[379] SECOND VATICAN ECUMENICAL COUNCIL, Dogmatic Constitution on the Church *Lumen Gentium*, 11.

faithfulness. This firm decision, which shapes a style of life, is an "interior requirement of the covenant of conjugal love",[380] since "a person who cannot choose to love for ever can hardly love for even a single day".[381] At the same time, such fidelity would be spiritually meaningless were it simply a matter of following a law with obedient resignation. Rather, it is a matter of the heart, into which God alone sees (cf. *Mt* 5:28). Every morning, on rising, we reaffirm before God our decision to be faithful, come what may in the course of the day. And all of us, before going to sleep, hope to wake up and continue this adventure, trusting in the Lord's help. In this way, each spouse is for the other a sign and instrument of the closeness of the Lord, who never abandons us: "Lo, I am with you always, to the close of the age" (*Mt* 28:20).

320. There comes a point where a couple's love attains the height of its freedom and becomes the basis of a healthy autonomy. This happens when each spouse realizes that the other is not his or her own, but has a much more important master, the one Lord. No one but God can presume to take over the deepest and most personal core of the loved one; he alone can be the ultimate centre of their life. At the same time, the principle of spiritual realism requires that one spouse not presume that the other can completely satisfy his or her needs. The spiritual journey of each - as Dietrich Bonhoeffer nicely put it - needs to help them to a certain "disillusionment" with regard to the other,[382] to stop expecting from that person something which is proper to the love of God alone. This demands an interior divestment. The space which each of the spouses makes exclusively for their personal relationship with God not only helps heal the hurts of life in common, but also enables the spouses to find in the love of God the deepest source of meaning in their own lives. Each day we have to invoke the help of the Holy Spirit to make this interior freedom possible.

---

[380] JOHN PAUL II, Apostolic Exhortation *Familiaris Consortio* (22 November 1981), 11: AAS 74 (1982), 93.

[381] ID., *Homily at Mass with Families,* Cordoba, Argentina (8 April 1987), 4: *Insegnamenti* X/1 (1987), 1161-1162.

[382] Cf. *Gemeinsames Leben*, Munich, 1973, p. 18. English: *Life Together*, New York, 1954, p. 27.

A SPIRITUALITY OF CARE, CONSOLATION AND INCENTIVE

321. "Christian couples are, for each other, for their children and for their relatives, co-operators of grace and witnesses of the faith".[383] God calls them to bestow life and to care for life. For this reason the family "has always been the nearest 'hospital'".[384] So let us care for one another, guide and encourage one another, and experience this as a part of our family spirituality. Life as a couple is a daily sharing in God's creative work, and each person is for the other a constant challenge from the Holy Spirit. God's love is proclaimed "through the living and concrete word whereby a man and the woman express their conjugal love".[385] The two are thus mutual reflections of that divine love which comforts with a word, a look, a helping hand, a caress, an embrace. For this reason "to want to form a family is to resolve to be a part of God's dream, to choose to dream with him, to want to build with him, to join him in this saga of building a world where no one will feel alone".[386]

322. All family life is a "shepherding" in mercy. Each of us, by our love and care, leaves a mark on the life of others; with Paul, we can say: "You are our letter of recommendation, written on your hearts... not with ink, but with the Spirit of the living God" (*2 Cor* 3:2-3). Each of us is a "fisher of men" (*Lk* 5:10) who in Jesus' name "casts the nets" (cf. *Lk* 5:5) for others, or a farmer who tills the fresh soil of those whom he or she loves, seeking to bring out the best in them. Marital fruitfulness involves helping others, for "to love anybody is to expect from him something which can neither be defined nor foreseen; it is at the same time in some way to make it possible for him to fulfil this expectation".[387] This is itself a way to worship God, who has sown so much good in others in the hope that we will help make it grow.

---

[383] SECOND VATICAN ECUMENICAL COUNCIL, Decree on the Apostolate of the Laity *Apostolicam Actuositatem*, 11.

[384] *Catechesis* (10 June 2015): *L'Osservatore Romano*, 11 June 2015, p. 8.

[385] JOHN PAUL II, Apostolic Exhortation *Familiaris Consortio* (22 November 1981), 12: AAS 74 (1982), 93.

[386] *Address at the Prayer Vigil of the Festival of Families*, Philadelphia (26 September 2015): *L'Osservatore Romano*, 28-29 September 2015, p. 6.

[387] GABRIEL MARCEL, *Homo Viator: prolégomènes à une métaphysique de l'espérance*, Paris, 1944, p. 66. English: *Homo Viator. An Introduction to a Metaphysics of Hope*, London, 1951, p. 49.

323. It is a profound spiritual experience to contemplate our loved ones with the eyes of God and to see Christ in them. This demands a freedom and openness which enable us to appreciate their dignity. We can be fully present to others only by giving fully of ourselves and forgetting all else. Our loved ones merit our complete attention. Jesus is our model in this, for whenever people approached to speak with him, he would meet their gaze, directly and lovingly (cf. *Mk* 10:21). No one felt overlooked in his presence, since his words and gestures conveyed the question: "What do you want me to do for you?" (*Mk* 10:51). This is what we experience in the daily life of the family. We are constantly reminded that each of those who live with us merits complete attention, since he or she possesses infinite dignity as an object of the Father's immense love. This gives rise to a tenderness which can "stir in the other the joy of being loved. Tenderness is expressed in a particular way by exercising loving care in treating the limitations of the other, especially when they are evident".[388]

324. Led by the Spirit, the family circle is not only open to life by generating it within itself, but also by going forth and spreading life by caring for others and seeking their happiness. This openness finds particular expression in hospitality,[389] which the word of God eloquently encourages: "Do not neglect to show hospitality to strangers, for thereby some have entertained angels unawares" (*Heb* 13:2). When a family is welcoming and reaches out to others, especially the poor and the neglected, it is "a symbol, witness and participant in the Church's motherhood".[390] Social love, as a reflection of the Trinity, is what truly unifies the spiritual meaning of the family and its mission to others, for it makes present the kerygma in all its communal imperatives. The family lives its spirituality precisely by being at one and the same time a domestic church and a vital cell for transforming the world.[391]

---

[388] *Relatio Finalis* 2015, 88.

[389] Cf. JOHN PAUL II, Apostolic Exhortation *Familiaris Consortio* (22 November 1981), 44: AAS 74 (1982), 136.

[390] *Ibid.*, 49: AAS 74 (1982), 141.

[391] For the social aspects of the family, cf. PONTIFICAL COUNCIL FOR JUSTICE AND PEACE, *Compendium of the Social Doctrine of the Church*, 248-254.

325. The teaching of the Master (cf. *Mt* 22:30) and Saint Paul (cf. *1 Cor* 7:29-31) on marriage is set - and not by chance - in the context of the ultimate and definitive dimension of our human existence. We urgently need to rediscover the richness of this teaching. By heeding it, married couples will come to see the deeper meaning of their journey through life. As this Exhortation has often noted, no family drops down from heaven perfectly formed; families need constantly to grow and mature in the ability to love. This is a neverending vocation born of the full communion of the Trinity, the profound unity between Christ and his Church, the loving community which is the Holy Family of Nazareth, and the pure fraternity existing among the saints of heaven. Our contemplation of the fulfilment which we have yet to attain also allows us to see in proper perspective the historical journey which we make as families, and in this way to stop demanding of our interpersonal relationships a perfection, a purity of intentions and a consistency which we will only encounter in the Kingdom to come. It also keeps us from judging harshly those who live in situations of frailty. All of us are called to keep striving towards something greater than ourselves and our families, and every family must feel this constant impulse. Let us make this journey as families, let us keep walking together. What we have been promised is greater than we can imagine. May we never lose heart because of our limitations, or ever stop seeking that fulness of love and communion which God holds out before us.

Prayer to the Holy Family

Jesus, Mary and Joseph,
in you we contemplate
the splendour of true love;
to you we turn with trust.

Holy Family of Nazareth,
grant that our families too
may be places of communion and prayer,
authentic schools of the Gospel
and small domestic churches.

Holy Family of Nazareth,
may families never again experience
violence, rejection and division;
may all who have been hurt or scandalized
find ready comfort and healing.

Holy Family of Nazareth,
make us once more mindful
of the sacredness and inviolability of the family,
and its beauty in God's plan.

Jesus, Mary and Joseph,
Graciously hear our prayer.
Amen.

Given in Rome, at Saint Peter's, during the Extraordinary Jubilee of Mercy, on 19 March, the Solemnity of Saint Joseph, in the year 2016, the fourth of my Pontificate.